DIVINE DESIGN

40 Days of Spiritual Makeover

By Sharla Fritz

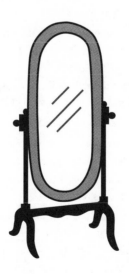

CONCORDIA PUBLISHING HOUSE · SAINT LOUIS

Published by Concordia Publishing House
3558 S. Jefferson Avenue, St. Louis, MO 63118-3968
1-800-325-3040 · www.cph.org

Text © 2010 Sharla Fritz

Interior art © Kathy Konkle/iStockphoto.com; © Cindy Hughes/Shutterstock, Inc.; © Tracie Andrews/
Shutterstock, Inc.; © Shutterstock, Inc.

3   4   5   6   7   8   9   10   19   18   17   16   15   14

Table of Contents

Introduction

Imagine. Cameras flash. Applause fills the room. Faces light up and mouths drop open. Cries of "You look fantastic!" and "I can't believe it's you!" reach your ears.

You take a few steps into the room. You slowly turn to show off your chic dress and point one toe to display your patent leather pumps. Friends rush forward and you hold out one perfectly manicured hand.

You have just participated in a fashion makeover. You look beautiful, polished, and radiant. For the moment, you feel like royalty.

While it might be exciting to experience a beauty makeover, that kind of transformation doesn't last long. By tomorrow, the perfectly styled hairdo will be flattened. By next week, the manicure will be chipped. By next month, the shoes will look scuffed. The elegant dress will last a little longer, but by next year, it will be out of date.

Divine Design: 40 Days of Spiritual Makeover will lead you through a different kind of transformation. This makeover will result in an alteration of your attitudes. A journey through these pages will, by God's grace, enable you to experience a renovation of character that will not become chipped, scuffed, or passé.

This makeover may not get you a spot on a reality TV show or land you on the cover of a magazine. Friends may not praise your new look. Your family may not stand up and applaud. However, those close to you will notice a transformation. You will recognize a difference in your spirit. Most of all, this makeover will be pleasing to God.

My hope is that you will trust God to work a change in your heart. Simply reading this book will not transform you. If you take the time to examine your life, read and believe God's Word, and permit the Holy Spirit to alter your heart, He will.

This book is designed to take you on an important, yet light-hearted, journey. It contains careful examination and study of God's Word. Because the Bible was written in Hebrew and Greek, we will sometimes explore the words of these original languages. The meaning of specific Greek or Hebrew words often helps to explain a passage or give a new point of view. This book also contains sometimes painful, sometimes amusing stories of my personal struggle to be conformed to God's image.

During each week in this eight-week study, you will consider a specific attitude or aspect of our spiritual makeover. The weekly chapters are divided into five daily readings and study guides. I hope that this format will help you develop a daily time with the Lord: time to read, reflect, study, and apply His Word to all aspects of your life. I encourage you to mark up your book. Underline or highlight passages that inspire or challenge you. Make notes in the margins. Write questions about things that are unclear or that you want to discuss with your group or your pastor.

A few tools are used consistently throughout the book:

What key lesson did you learn today? Each day, you will be asked this question. Your answer can be from the reading, from the Bible passages examined, or from a thought that God revealed to you during your time with Him. Answering this question will help you to choose one idea or concept to inspire your day.

Memory verse. Each day, you will be instructed to write out the memory verse for the week. The act of writing out the words will help you to commit them to heart. You might also write the verse on a card to carry in your purse or on a sticky note to display by the sink or computer monitor. Storing God's Word in our hearts is one of the most effective ways of changing our attitudes.

Study Styles. Every week, the Study Styles section will examine a different method of exploring the Bible. Hopefully, these techniques will help you to get more out of your Bible study. Once you have tried these Study Styles, you may want to use them with other Bible passages.

Meaningful Makeover. The Bible is full of fascinating people, amazing stories, and thought-provoking quotes, but if that is all we get out of it, we have missed the point. In the Bible, God speaks to us, instructs us, and guides us. The weekly Meaningful Makeover section directs you to apply God's Word to all aspects of your life. The power of His Gospel can change you, transform you, and make you new.

Maybe cameras won't flash. Applause may not fill the room. Mouths of friends probably won't drop open in amazement. But a spiritual makeover will transform your heart. In God's grace, your inner beauty will shine. A gentle and quiet spirit will emerge. You will still feel like royalty, because you are a daughter of the King. None of us can spend time with Him and not be changed.

—Sharla Fritz

Suggestions for Small-Group Participants

1. Begin small-group time with prayer.

2. Everyone should feel free to express her thoughts. Things shared with the group should remain confidential unless you have received permission to share it outside your group.

3. If your meeting time does not allow you to discuss all of the questions for the week, the leader should choose the questions most meaningful to the group. I suggest that every session include discussion of the first question, Study Styles, and Meaningful Makeover.

4. Keep encouraging everyone to memorize the weekly memory verse. Say this verse together at the end of the session.

5. Close with prayer time, sharing concerns and prayer requests.

WEEK ONE

WHAT WE WEAR—
Wardrobe Woes

Memory Verse

You have heard about Him and were taught in Him, as the truth is in Jesus, to put off your old self, which is ... corrupt through deceitful desires, and to be renewed in the spirit of your minds, and to put on the new self, created after the likeness of God in true righteousness and holiness.

Ephesians 4:21–24

Day One
◇◇◇◇◇◇◇◇◇◇◇◇◇◇◇◇◇◇◇◇◇◇
Wardrobe Woes

Strength and dignity are her clothing,
and she laughs at the time to come.
Proverbs 31:25

I have a confession to make. I have a weakness for makeover shows. It is simply fascinating to me to watch the renovation of a room, a house, or a person—all accomplished in one hour and with no work on my part! Carpenters restore old homes and bring them back to their former glory. Decorators replace peeling paint and faded curtains with fresh new colors and updated window treatments. Professional organizers convert overstuffed garages into systematized and color-coded storage units.

I am particularly fascinated by the makeover program *What Not to Wear.* In each episode, friends and family nominate one poor, unsuspecting person for a fashion makeover. First, camera crews secretly film the person in his or her most unflattering outfits. Then the fashion team confronts the nominee, often ridiculing the style-deficient individual. The wardrobe consultants proceed to show him or her which styles and colors look best on her and finally present the fashion-challenged person with a generous budget to shop for a new wardrobe. When I watch the show, I am amazed at the transformation that can be accomplished by simply changing the length of a skirt, the cut of a jacket, or the colors worn.

I have always liked fashionable clothes, although I continually struggle to look stylish. My sister and I joke that we are one fashion step behind, because we grew up in northern Wisconsin in a time when trends seemed to lag behind those in fashion centers such as New York and Los Angeles. We tend not to embrace a new style until it's on the way out.

I certainly could have been nominated as a fashion-challenged participant on *What Not to Wear.* I admit that I have worn some horrendous outfits—especially in my younger years! One particular outfit that would make today's top ten worst-dressed list was a hot pink Easter dress plastered with six-inch white and yellow daisies. A matching double-knit coat and hat completed the ensemble! At the time, I thought I looked pretty good, especially since I matched my mother. We were quite a pair!

In those days, we watched our pennies and made most of our clothes from material purchased from Herberger's bargain basement. Sometimes we found attractive fabric, like a camel and forest-green cotton plaid I used to sew a skirt. However, a few yards of peach-colored double-knit became a dress that stood out like a costume. Other fashion mistakes included the electric-green bodysuit I made in seventh grade and the purple corduroy bell-bottoms I designed in eighth grade, all with fabric from the bargain basement.

Budget considerations dictated our wardrobes more than anything else. In sixth grade, I remember needing a new winter coat—an essential in northern Wisconsin. My mother took me to a sale at a local clothing store known for quality merchandise. We found a beautiful raspberry-red plaid wool coat that was warm and luxurious. There was only one problem: it was a ladies size 12! I was nowhere near that size at the time, but my mother was certain I would grow into it. (In fact, I never did quite grow into that lovely garment.) I remember sitting at my desk with my coat on one morning as we waited to go out for recess, when the girl behind me looked at my raspberry number and asked, "What is *that?*"

As I matured, I improved at choosing clothes that fit and flatter, but I still make mistakes. Not so long ago, I decided to sew a shirt and skirt from matching fabric. Shirt dresses were in style, and I thought that sewing it in two pieces would make it more versatile because I could wear each piece with other separates. But my frugality got in the way again, and I purchased a print fabric from the clearance pile. Never mind that it was a decorator fabric; I was sure it would look wonderful. When I finished the ensemble, however, I looked like I was wearing curtains. Now where were those television wardrobe consultants when I needed them?

Proverbs 31 describes a godly woman dressed in her best: "Strength and dignity are her clothing, and she laughs at the time to come" (v. 25). Although I aimed for the image of strength and dignity, I often dressed in the cheap and chintzy. Instead of laughing at the days to come, I ended up laughing at my choices.

God is not terribly interested in our wardrobe selections. Although He certainly desires that we dress modestly, I doubt He cares if we wear boot-cut jeans or pleated trousers, a button-down shirt or a turtleneck. He is, however, concerned about how we clothe our character. In Christ, He loves us just as we are, but He sees our potential for more. He desires to work a spiritual makeover in our hearts. He alone can give our souls strength and dignity, power and poise. He is the only fashion consultant able to achieve a makeover miracle in our hearts. Through His Word, He can transform our hearts from a fearful, prideful, or vengeful state into hearts clothed in joy, peace, and love. Through His Sacraments, He transforms us, and our signature look will be a trust in His goodness that enables us to laugh with joy at the days to come.

So let's open ourselves up for a spiritual makeover. Let's discover what God wants to toss out of our character closets and what design He desires for our souls. Are you willing to nominate yourself for God's makeover show?

Dear Father in heaven, I thank You that You love me as I am, yet You desire to make my image shine as You work a spiritual makeover in my heart. Help me to be willing to throw out the old, unattractive clothing that wraps my spirit. Give me Your strength and dignity and the ability to laugh at the days to come. In Jesus' name. Amen.

Day One
Wardrobe Workout

1. Pretend Stacy and Clinton from *What Not to Wear* are coming to look in your closet! What wouldn't you want them to see? Pull out an item that has seen better days but that you still wear. Ask yourself why you keep it. If you are doing this study in a small group, bring this item to the meeting and discuss why we hold on to things that are not attractive.

2. "Strength and dignity are her clothing, and she laughs at the time to come" (Proverbs 31:25). *Strength* can be defined as "the power to resist strain." *Dignity* presents a picture of calmness and poise. Describe how the characteristics of strength and dignity could improve your everyday life.

3. What key lesson did you learn today? In the space below, write something God taught you that can make a difference in your life.

4. Our memory verse for this week is Ephesians 4:21–24: "You have heard about Him and were taught in Him, as the truth is in Jesus, to put off your old self, which is . . . corrupt through deceitful desires, and to be renewed in the spirit of your minds, and to put on the new self, created after the likeness of God in true righteousness and holiness." To help you memorize this passage, write it out in the space below.

Day Two

◇◇◇◇◇◇◇◇◇◇◇◇◇◇◇◇◇◇◇◇◇◇◇◇◇◇◇◇◇◇◇◇◇◇

A More Significant Makeover

Your beauty should not come from outward adornment, such as
braided hair and the wearing of gold jewelry and fine clothes.
Instead, it should be that of your inner self, the unfading beauty of
a gentle and quiet spirit, which is of great worth in God's sight.
1 Peter 3:3–4 NIV

Let's admit it: many women spend a lot of time and money on their appearance. We take care to choose jewelry, clothing, and hairstyles that will help us look our best. Tiffany sells millions of dollars of jewelry every year. On Forbes.com, financial analysts claim that Americans spent more than $87 billion on clothing in 2008. One British Web site estimated that the average woman in Great Britain spends the equivalent of almost two years of her life washing and styling her hair.

As we read Peter's words to the women of his day, it is clear that the focus on fashion is not a modern trend. Peter instructed his Jewish and Gentile readers to turn away from expensive clothing and accessories (1 Peter 3:3). It seems that even in the 60s (and that's AD 60, not the 1960s), women were concerned about having the latest hairdo and trendiest clothing. Perhaps the must-have item of the AD 65 fall season was an "Andrew" veil or a "Thomas" tunic. However, Peter was urging first-century women not to bother themselves with outward fashion trends. They were to cultivate inner beauty—a gentle and quiet spirit.

Peter is speaking to us today too. At a time when styles seem to change faster than traffic lights, we are to concern ourselves with the ageless fashion of our souls. While our culture encourages spending millions on clothes, jewelry, and hairstyles, as God's daughters, we are advised to use our resources to cultivate inner beauty. Instead of searching for the latest style in jackets or the trendiest bag, we are instructed to seek unchanging gentleness and enduring quietness.

In Galatians 5:22–23, Paul describes the fruit of the Spirit: "love, joy, peace, patience, kindness, goodness, faithfulness, gentleness, self-control," and says, "against such things there is no law," meaning that there is no restraint to these qualities. In the next verse, we read that "those who belong to Christ Jesus have crucified the flesh with its passions and desires" (v. 24). In other words, we completely surrender our emotions to Christ. I admit that surrender and acceptance are not always my first responses to God's actions in my life. As I grow in my trust in His goodness and His love for me, I gain a peace that will never go out of style. As my relationship with my loving Savior matures, I experience a serenity that will always make a fashion statement.

The Greek word for *quiet* means "tranquil, undisturbed." Fashion trends may come and go, but my spirit can remain steadfast in the Prince of Peace. No matter what complications come my way, I can continue in tranquility because Christ calms my soul.

Why should we pursue inner beauty rather than strive for physical attractiveness? I see three reasons:

- Inner beauty is more fulfilling. The beauty that comes from within is ultimately more satisfying than any external change we make in our appearance. Although cosmetic companies may try to convince me otherwise, no beauty cream will change my life. A fresh hairstyle may make me look younger and earn compliments, but it will not give me peace. Fashionable new pumps may give me a spring in my step, but will they change my outlook on life? (Okay, for footwear fanciers like me, that point might be debatable.)

  But seriously, think of the transformation you would see in your life if you could reduce the worry that clouds your mind, remove the envy that robs your joy, or eliminate the bitterness that ties your heart in knots.

- Inner beauty is unfading. A gentle and quiet spirit bestows an "unfading beauty" (1 Peter 3:4 NIV). Favorite hairstyles grow out. Our best sweaters shrink or pill. Jewelry tarnishes with age. On the other hand, trust in God's goodness and tranquility in Christ not only endure but they also increase with time. Peter tells us that "this is the way the holy women of the past who put their hope in God used to make themselves beautiful" (v. 5 NIV). Think of the truly beautiful women you admire, those who shine with an unshakable confidence in a loving Lord no matter what comes their way. That beauty is attainable at any age.

  There is nothing wrong with wearing beautiful and fashionable clothes, but God wants to shift our attention away from what designers are creating for the upcoming season and what fashion editors are promoting as the latest styles. He directs us to find the finest fashions, discover His spiritual style, and pinpoint which pieces are truly timeless.

- Inner beauty is precious to God. We may turn heads when we walk down the street in a smart new suit. A Gucci bag may incite admiration from our friends. Co-workers may ooh and aah over a new diamond necklace. But how do we please our Savior? With our "inner self, the unfading beauty of a gentle and quiet spirit" (v. 4 NIV). A "quiet spirit" will make God smile and bring Him pleasure. Unshakable hope in His goodness will land you on the cover of *Heavenly Vogue*.

So while it may be fun to impress others with our savvy fashion sense, let's set our sights on pleasing the Wardrobe Consultant who really matters.

> *Heavenly Father, please forgive me for the times I have been too concerned about fancy hairstyles, expensive jewelry, or beautiful clothes. Help me to concentrate on inner beauty. Give me the gentle and quiet spirit that is so precious to You. In Jesus' name and for His sake. Amen.*

Day Two
Wardrobe Workout

1. How do you define *inner beauty*? What are some characteristics of women you know who shine from the inside out?

2. Read Ephesians 4:22–32.

   a. Paul tells us to "put off" certain behaviors and to "put on" others. Why do you think he used this imagery of putting off and putting on?

b. We take off and put on clothing. How do clothing metaphors help you to understand the transformation God wants to work in your life?

c. Ephesians 4:22 (NIV) states, "Your old self . . . is being corrupted by its deceitful desires." Using a dictionary, define the following:

deceitful _____

desires _____

Now describe "deceitful desires" in your own words and explain how these desires can corrupt us.

3. What key lesson did you learn today?

4. Write out our memory verse for this week: "You have heard about Him and were taught in Him, as the truth is in Jesus, to put off your old self, which is . . . corrupt through deceitful desires, and to be renewed in the spirit of your minds, and to put on the new self, created after the likeness of God in true

righteousness and holiness" (Ephesians 4:21–24). Read a phrase, then cover it and write it. Try to write as much of the verse as you can without looking.

Day Three

Essential Garments

I will greatly rejoice in the LORD;
my soul shall exult in my God,
for He has clothed me with the garments of salvation;
He has covered me with the robe of righteousness,
as a bridegroom decks himself like a priest with a beautiful
headdress, and as a bride adorns herself with her jewels.
Isaiah 61:10

Where do we start? How do we begin our spiritual makeover? We know that our miracle-working Wardrobe Consultant, the Holy Spirit, is prepared to give us a fresh, new image. We are ready to nominate ourselves for our Lord's makeover show. We realize that inner beauty is more lasting and satisfying than anything we see in the pages of *Vogue* or *Glamour*.

When a fashion expert plans a wardrobe for a client, she starts with basic pieces and essential garments. Fashion magazines tell us that key pieces are clothes in neutral colors that act as building blocks for multiple outfits. However, our divine Wardrobe Consultant is designing a different look for us.

The prophet Isaiah tells us that God gives us the most essential garments in our wardrobe: "He has clothed me with the garments of salvation; He has covered me with the robe of righteousness" (Isaiah 61:10). The garments of salvation and the robe of righteousness are the must-have pieces, not just for a season, but for eternity! Without these indispensable articles of clothing, we cannot enter God's kingdom. Because of His great love for us, our gracious Father dresses us in the robe of righteousness when we receive the gift of faith in Christ our Savior through water and the Word. He wraps us in the garments of salvation and clothes our hearts with His Spirit and His love.

In the Old Testament, the prophet Zechariah tells of a vision he received about a significant wardrobe change. In the vision, Joshua, the high priest, stood in the presence of the Lord, wearing filthy, soiled clothes. Satan was right there with them, making accusations against Joshua. But God Himself interrupted Satan and rebuked him. He instructed the angel to remove the dirty clothes and dress Joshua in royal robes. He said to Joshua, "See, I have taken away your sin, and I will put rich garments on you" (Zechariah 3:4 NIV).

I imagine myself in Joshua's place. I have come before the Lord, and Satan doesn't miss a stitch—he's right there to accuse me. I hang my head in shame because I know what he says is true. I have blown it so many times and in so many ways with my family, my friends, and my co-workers. I've been selfish, impatient, and unkind. Other times I have been well-meaning but lazy. I look down and I see my grimy clothes. The stains are there for everyone to see. But Christ's voice pierces the air and ends Satan's finger-pointing session. "Stop, Satan! I have forgiven her! I have snatched her from damnation!" He looks at me with eyes of love and instructs an angel to remove my muddied garments. The angel peels away the clothes that I have been ashamed to wear. The dirt that has clung to me disappears. Then the angel brings a rich, beautiful robe and puts it on me—I cannot even do this for myself. More than my clothes have been changed. I am no longer grimy and guilty, but clean, unsoiled, and forgiven. God's mercy removes my dirt, His transforming grace washes away my stains, and His robe of righteousness covers my guilt. Tears trickle out of my eyes in joy.

Don't you love how the Lord works? He knew we needed that robe of righteousness. He understood the suit of salvation was an essential garment in our wardrobe.

This fashion item is priceless; we cannot buy it at Target or Wal-Mart, at Macy's or J. C. Penney, not even at Saks Fifth Avenue or Bloomingdale's. Jesus already purchased this garment for us with His own blood when He died on the cross for us. Now He holds it out to us, inviting us to slip our arms into the sleeves. As we do, that immaculate white robe of salvation wraps us in His mercy and grace. We stand before Him clean and forgiven.

Perhaps all this talk of robes of righteousness and garments of salvation is new to you. Don't worry. God's salvation is available to everyone. He eagerly desires to give you His righteousness, that is, the state of being right with God. In Christ's death and resurrection, the barrier between us and God was removed forever. We are able to know Him personally.

Perhaps you have heard about God's salvation and His righteousness all your life. Perhaps you're like me, and you received the robe of righteousness at your Baptism. Sometimes I do not fully appreciate this priceless gift of salvation because I have possessed it for a long time. It's like the Christmas sweater I was thrilled to receive but that now sits in a drawer, forgotten. Often I neglect to thank my Savior for enduring unspeakable pain, sacrificing His life for me, and defeating my ultimate enemy, eternal damnation, by rising from the grave.

Let's take the time to express our gratefulness to God who, is ready to give us the essential garments of salvation; to Jesus, who paid the price for the clothes that cover our sin, and to the Holy Spirit, who works righteousness in our hearts.

Almighty God, thank You for giving me salvation; I know there is nothing I could have done to earn it on my own. Forgive me when I have not treasured Your costly gift. Precious Jesus, thank You for paying the price for my sinfulness through Your death and resurrection. Holy Spirit, thank You for clothing me in righteousness, covering the stains of my sin and guilt. Amen.

Day Three

◇◇◇◇◇◇◇◇◇◇◇◇◇◇◇◇◇◇◇◇◇◇◇

Wardrobe Workout

1. Isaiah 61:10 reads, "I will greatly rejoice in the LORD; my soul shall exult in my God, for He has clothed me with the garments of salvation; He has covered me with the robe of righteousness." Read the following and check all that apply to you:

   _____ I have not received the robe of righteousness.

   _____ I have not received the robe of righteousness, but I would like to.

   _____ I have received the robe of righteousness.

   _____ My spiritual character has not changed much in recent years.

   _____ Lately, God has worked a renewal of my character.

   _____ I desire to continue the renovation of my soul.

   Explain your answers.

2. Read the following verses and write down the spiritual clothing mentioned.

   a. Job 29:14 _____

   b. Psalm 30:11 _____

   c. Isaiah 52:1 _____

   d. Luke 24:49 _____

   Which of these garments do you wear all the time? Which ones would you like to wear more often?

3. What key lesson did you learn today?

4. Write out this week's memory verse. Try not to peek!

Day Four

<><><><><><><><><><><><>

A Fresh Image

Put on then, as God's chosen ones, holy and beloved, compassionate
hearts, kindness, humility, meekness, and patience.
Colossians 3:12

Slipping into that robe of righteousness is an eternal makeover and the beginning of a spiritual renovation. While we live here on earth, we still have access to the closet of our old life. From time to time, we may be tempted to pull out items that belong in the past. God wants to give us a fresh new image, inside and out.

Because I am a confirmed sweater-holic, my husband threatens to curb my addiction. "When the number of sweaters reaches triple digits," he jokes, "you will have to part with some of them." Actually, my closet and drawer space dictate that I reduce my collection long before my warm, fuzzy garments number one hundred. (But wait, my daughter has moved out! Should I start using her closet?)

Just as I comply with my husband's encouragement to purge out-of-date and seldom-worn sweaters from my wardrobe, God's Law reminds me that I need to clear unattractive habits and attitudes from my spiritual attire. When the Bible talks about the clothing of our inner spirit, it frequently encourages us to take something off before we put on something else. With the help of the Holy Spirit, I'm able to tackle this task. Because I wear the robe of righteousness Christ gives me, I can clean out my closet.

The British *What Not to Wear* ladies, Trinny Woodall and Susannah Constantine, write, "Looking stylish is as much about knowing what not to wear as it is about knowing what suits you" (Woodall and Constantine, p. 6). An expert wardrobe consultant will surely tell me which styles make my hips look like ham hocks or my thighs like sausages. In the same way, the Bible shows me which attitudes are unflattering and unattractive so that I can eliminate them from my wardrobe. In this way, I make room for the garments that suit my new image in Christ.

The apostle Paul encourages a spiritual makeover in Colossians:

> Put to death therefore what is earthly in you: sexual immorality,
> impurity, passion, evil desire, and covetousness, which is idolatry. On

account of these the wrath of God is coming. In these you too once walked, when you were living in them. But now you must put them all away: anger, wrath, malice, slander, and obscene talk from your mouth. Do not lie to one another, seeing that you have put off the old self with its practices and have put on the new self, which is being renewed in knowledge after the image of its creator. Here there is not Greek and Jew, circumcised and uncircumcised, barbarian, Scythian, slave, free; but Christ is all, and in all.

Put on then, as God's chosen ones, holy and beloved, compassionate hearts, kindness, humility, meekness, and patience, bearing with one another and, if one has a complaint against another, forgiving each other; as the Lord has forgiven you, so you also must forgive. (Colossians 3:5–13)

Paul tells me to abandon my old way of life, which has habits and patterns of behavior that need to be stripped off. My old, worn character may have a comfortable routine to which I am accustomed, but that does not suit my new existence. My natural inclination may be toward worry in times of stress or toward anger when I don't get my way. The fashion of my speech may sometimes include harsh words or so-called harmless gossip. Television commercials and that item the neighbors just bought may shape my desires. "Little white lies" and "looking out for number one" seem to fit naturally. Yet all of these attitudes need to be thrown away. This doesn't mean that I will never make a mistake, never slip up, or never go back to my old conduct. But it does mean that I will no longer make those behaviors habitual. I will not continue to do them unthinkingly, day in and day out.

My Creator fashioned me in His image, but my inherited sin and my own shortcomings have smeared that image. As I allow the Holy Spirit to work in my life, He restores a godly likeness. He will help me remove the old way of life and put on the new. He will guide me to a deeper knowledge of my Maker. The original Greek word for *knowledge* here in Colossians indicates a knowledge that powerfully influences one's life. As I study His Word, receive His Holy Supper, and become better acquainted with the One who fashioned me, He will change me to look more like Him. My image will reflect the image of Christ.

It doesn't matter what I look like before my makeover. The Greeks and uncircumcised people that Paul mentions in Colossians 3:11 were considered unclean by the Jews. My own character may be soiled and dirty. In Paul's time, the barbarians and Scythians were seen as uncivilized and crude. "Coarse and unsophisticated" might describe my current spiritual wardrobe. In the first century, slaves were tightly bound to their masters. The garments of my human nature may be uncomfortably snug and constricting. But because I live in baptismal grace, Christ in me will free my spirit to live for Him.

Because God loves me dearly and has chosen to give me a clean, new image, He will help me select clothing that fits my fresh, new look. He will exchange honesty for lies, compassion for anger, and kindness for malice. Humility, gentleness, and patience become wardrobe staples, replacing the old standbys of impurity, evil desires, and greed. Christ will help me to wear forgiveness instead of rage. His love is the belt that will tie the whole ensemble together.

Heavenly Father, I know that my sins and shortcomings have smeared the image that You desire for me. Please remove all the unattractive habits and attitudes from my life and give me new ones that suit my new image in Christ. Amen.

Day Four
◇◇◇◇◇◇◇◇◇◇◇◇◇◇◇◇◇◇◇◇
Wardrobe Workout

1. We all hang on to attitudes or behaviors that are not becoming. List some reasons why it is so difficult to accomplish change in our spiritual closets.

2. Read Colossians 3:5–13 again. Which verse spoke most clearly to you? How might you respond to Paul's encouragement to put on Christ in your daily life?

3. What key lesson did you learn today?

4. Write out this week's memory verse. No peeking!

◇◇◇◇◇◇◇◇◇◇◇◇
Study Styles

There are various ways to study the Bible. In this section, we will consider a different technique for exploring God's Word—a new study style.

One good way to get the most out of your Bible study is to make charts of what you have learned. Using Ephesians 4:22–32, make a chart listing **What Not to Wear** and **What to Wear.**

What Not to Wear	What to Wear

Now circle the characteristics you are currently wearing!

Day Five

◇◇◇◇◇◇◇◇◇◇◇◇◇◇◇

Spiritual Style

*Do not be conformed to this world, but be transformed by the
renewal of your mind, that by testing you may discern what is the
will of God, what is good and acceptable and perfect.*
Romans 12:2

With my hot pink daisy dress and my raspberry-red plaid coat, there was no doubt that when I was young, I needed a *What Not to Wear* advisor. As an adult, I realized that not only did my walk-in closet at home need a makeover, but my inner character did too! I had a wardrobe full of unattractive attitudes that I would pull out and wear from time to time. Worry was a favorite accessory that I carried everywhere. Pride was like the high school prom dress that I could never bring myself to purge from my closet. Controlling behavior became a uniform I put on every day. It was time for a spiritual makeover!

The quality of my character, the shape of my values, and the fashion of my spirit are all more significant than owning an Armani suit or a Gucci bag. The attitudes I choose to wear define who I am more than my wardrobe. Kindness and compassion are more attractive than the most professional power suit and patent-leather pumps. Humility and patience will be in style much longer than boot-cut jeans and trapeze jackets. Truthfulness and graciousness will ultimately impress more people than expensive designer labels and luxurious fabrics.

Perhaps you picked up this book because you, too, recognize that the fashion of your character needs a makeover. If you feel that it's time to rid your spiritual wardrobe of everything that is not God-pleasing, then join me in altering attitudes that don't do a thing for our image, old thinking that binds and pinches, and characteristics that never were in style.

In the process, we will make a fresh start and find room in our closets for the values that God wants in our lives. The authors of *Nothing to Wear?* explain the advantages of cleaning our clothes closets:

> The purpose behind editing your wardrobe is to achieve "wardrobe
> clarity." Done correctly, it is a process of redefinition and renewal,
> not just cleaning out the clutter. (Garza and Lupo, p. 61)

In the same way, our spiritual garments may need editing and our character may require renewal.

Sometimes clothing is just a habit. In the past, I wore navy slacks all the time, because they coordinated with many different color tops. When I went shopping for new shirts, I automatically looked for items that went with navy. Navy became my routine—until I discovered that it is not a very flattering color on me! In the same way, I may carry my bag of worries every day, simply because it is now a habit. I'm accustomed to dragging my anxiety around day after day, and I'm not aware of a better accessory to use!

Just as I didn't know that navy was not a good color for me until I consulted a color expert, we may not be aware that we routinely wear character qualities that are unattractive and project a negative image. Thankfully, we all have our own spiritual wardrobe consultant to show us the proper attire for our souls: God! Our awesome Creator made each one of us in a unique and special way and designed the garments we need to be at our best. God's Word gives us clear instruction regarding the apparel He wants us to wear.

According to the ladies of *What Not to Wear*, "Once you really understand what not to wear the path to chic-dom becomes a piece of cake" (Woodall and Constantine, p. 7). Let's become spiritually chic as we learn what to wear and what to discard. Let's allow the Holy Spirit to work in our hearts to expose our wardrobe flaws gently and to give us the garments that will help our new image shine.

> *Holy Spirit, I realize that the attitudes and habits I wear are*
> *more important than my wardrobe. Work in my heart. Show me*
> *where I need to change. Let me see the character qualities that*
> *You want me to wear. In Jesus' name. Amen.*

Day Five
◇◇◇◇◇◇◇◇◇◇◇◇◇◇◇◇◇◇◇◇◇◇
Wardrobe Workout

1. What does a spiritual makeover mean to you? What changes would you like to see in your life?

2. Paul says we are "to be made new in the attitude of your minds" (Ephesians 4:23 NIV). The word translated as "attitude" in the NIV is *pneuma,* which can mean spirit, human rational mind or mental disposition. Discuss how our attitudes can influence our actions and govern our souls.

3. What key lesson did you learn today?

4. Write out this week's memory verse, Ephesians 4:21–24, from memory.

◇◇◇◇◇◇◇◇◇◇◇◇◇◇◇◇◇◇◇◇◇◇◇◇◇◇◇◇◇◇
Meaningful Makeover

Bible study is more than learning facts and terms. God's Word is living and active and transforms our lives. Look at the chart you completed yesterday (page 28). Choose one item you circled in the **What Not to Wear** column that you would like to toss or one item not circled in the **What to Wear** column that you would like to add to your life. What are some steps you can take to make this a reality?

(Example: In my life, I would like to add speech that builds others up. One practical step I can take is to encourage each member of my family every day.)

Write a prayer asking your divine Designer to help you edit out the unattractive behavior or to clothe you with one that will reflect your new image in Christ!

Remember to bring the clothing item from Day One
to your group's meeting!

WEEK TWO

CONTROLLING BEHAVIOR—
Hang Up the
Field Marshal Uniform

Memory Verse

I delight to do Your will, O my God; Your law is within my heart.

Psalm 40:8

Day One
◇◇◇◇◇◇◇◇◇◇
In Control

Submit yourselves therefore to God.
James 4:7

I'm a recovering control freak. I like to be in charge. Although I've never been in the military, one outfit in which I often paraded around was a high-ranking commander's uniform. I didn't earn my stripes in boot camp or work my way up through the ranks; I simply donned the attire of an officer, with lots of medals, bars, and stars!

Now that I think about it, I may have inherited this uniform. It's possible that I didn't have much control over becoming a control freak, because I come from a long line of controllers. My grandfather was a stubborn guy who was *never* wrong. One day while driving, my husband and I saw a bumper sticker that described him perfectly: "You can always tell a German, but you can't tell him much." (Perhaps you are nodding your head, but substituting Irish or Italian.)

Next, there's my mom. She admits she likes to share her "advice" with people. One Christmas, my daughter made personalized wooden gift tags for everyone. On Grandma's tag she painted, "Everyone is entitled to my opinion." When my mother first saw the tag, she said, "What does this mean? I'm not sure I like this!" However, good sport that my mom is, she soon started carrying around the little tag in her purse, showing it to everyone, and using it as a license! Mom once told me about a church sign she likes: "For peace of mind, resign as the general manager of the universe." Nevertheless, she confessed that she sometimes finds it difficult to put that suggestion into practice.

And then there's the fact that I am the oldest of my siblings, the firstborn. Isn't it a well-known fact that big sisters were put on earth to boss around their younger siblings?

The desire to be in control can make one difficult to live with, and regrettably, it took me a while before I realized that. You see, I like to plan things out, keep things organized, and have all my ducks in a row. I organize my clothes by color, my kitchen utensils by use, and my books alphabetically by author's last name. My husband is much more easy-going. When we got married, he moved in with containers that included textbooks, car parts, and clothing—all in the same box!

My sister-in-law, a human resources specialist, once told us about a personality test she was using at the corporation where she worked. She was excited about it and guessed how each of us might be classified. When she came to me, she said, "Now, Sharla, you would surely be called a Field Marshal." I wasn't sure I liked that! How could she compare me to a bossy military commander who ordered troops? But I took her assessment to heart and tried to change my ways. Although it was painful at first, I began using phrases such as "You decide" and "It's your choice." I must have improved, because a few years later, my sister-in-law commented, "Sharla, you've become much less of a field marshal in your old age." Now, I'm glad I've improved and become less of a control freak; however, I'm not too thrilled about that "old age" comment.

How was I able to get rid of that field marshal jacket? How was it possible to step out of the commander's uniform?

In order to change, I needed to remember that God is the one wearing the field marshal suit. James 4:7 says, "Submit yourselves therefore to God." The Greek word for *submit* is *hupotassō*, which is primarily a military term meaning "to rank under." According to *Vine's Expository Dictionary of Old and New Testament Words*, in this context, the word means "to subject oneself, to obey, be subject to." In other words, we are to place ourselves willingly in a rank lower than God. We are to be willing to obey Him and to do whatever He commands or wishes. Instead of donning the authoritative commander's uniform, I must be willing to wear the battle fatigues of the common soldier. Trendiness of camouflage print aside, fatigues are not terribly fashionable, but they show that we are in the army. They indicate our place in the chain of command. I have no bars on my shoulders, no stripes on my sleeve. I don't give orders; I take them.

The first step in trading in the commanding officer's uniform is to let God be in charge of my life. This is totally different from my natural inclination to want to be in control and to direct situations according to my wishes. But when I acknowledge God's power, His omnipotence, and His sovereignty in the world and in my life, I experience a greater happiness than when I delude myself about being in charge. I acknowledged that God's plans surpass my own, that He desires what is best for me, and that when I am willing to let Him lead, He will guide me to a life of purpose and satisfaction far greater than anything I could design.

> *Lord Jesus, I admit that I have not always treated You as Lord*
> *of my life. Too often I have tried to be in control. I ask You now to*

be the ruler of my life. Help me to understand that Your ways are even better than my hopes and wishes. Amen.

Day One
Wardrobe Workout

1. Look in your closet for an outfit that gives you a feeling of authority or control. Perhaps you are or were in the military and have a uniform hanging there. Do you have a power suit or a vibrant jacket that boosts your self-confidence? Maybe you have one particular outfit that looks terrific on you and always reaps compliments. Describe the outfit and the way it makes you feel. Bring the outfit or a photograph of you in it to your group's next meeting. Talk about how the clothes we wear can affect how we perceive ourselves.

2. Which uniform would you rather wear: the commander's uniform or the private's uniform? Why?

3. If God is in charge of my life, I must obey His commands. Read the following passages. What does God have to say about obedience and following His commands?

1 Samuel 15:22 _____

_____

_____

Isaiah 48:18 _____

_____

_____

Jeremiah 7:23 _____

_____

_____

John 14:21 _____

_____

_____

1 John 5:3 _____

_____

_____

4. What key lesson did you learn today?

5. Our memory verse for this week is Psalm 40:8: "I delight to do Your will, O my God; Your law is within my heart." To help you memorize this verse, write it out in the space below.

Day Two

◇◇◇◇◇◇◇◇◇◇◇◇◇◇◇◇◇◇

Disown Yourself

If anyone would come after Me, let him deny himself and take up
his cross daily and follow Me.
Luke 9:23

Boot camp. Push-ups. Sit-ups. Long marches with heavy backpacks. Sergeants barking orders to new recruits who realize their lives are no longer their own.

Jesus is not a demanding, callous sergeant, but as Lord of our lives, He requests that we report for spiritual boot camp. He informed His disciples that following Him meant denying themselves.

What does denying myself involve? Sometimes such denial means I have to give up Chicago-style pizza, dark chocolate, and blueberry cheesecake so I can fit into my favorite jeans.

God, however, has something else in mind. He wants me to trust Him enough to transfer ownership of myself to my Commanding Officer: Jesus, my Lord. He asks me to relinquish the rights to my earthly interests, forget about my preferences, and surrender my life to Him. "If you love Me," Jesus says in John 14:15, "you will keep my commandments."

In 1 Samuel 15:22, we read that "to obey is better than sacrifice." Oswald Chambers had a lot to say on the subject of surrender. My copy of his devotional, *My Utmost for His Highest*, has many passages highlighted such as this one:

> To become one with Jesus Christ, a person must be willing not only to give up sin, but also to surrender his whole way of looking at things. . . . Once we have done that, the Spirit of God will show us what we need to surrender next. Along each step of this process, we will have to give up our claims to our rights to ourselves. (Chambers, March 8)

Okay, this sounds scary! Give up control over myself? Surrender the right to my own decisions? How could anyone else possibly know what was best for me? I wanted to reach back into the closet and put on that field marshal uniform!

Chambers also wrote, "He must deny his right to himself, and he must realize who Jesus Christ is before he will bring himself to do it. Beware of refusing to go to the funeral of your own independence" (Chambers, December 9). When I take off that commander's uniform, I bury my independence. When I put on the plain uniform of a private, I relinquish the freedom to have my own way. When I sign up for God's boot camp, I agree to sacrifice my right to myself. But this is terribly difficult to do if I don't know the character of my Commanding Officer. I cannot bring myself to hold a funeral for my independence until I understand who Jesus Christ is. I can't give up control until I realize, "Duh. God made me: He knows me better than I know myself! Jesus loves me: He proved that by dying for me. God is good: He wants only what is best for me."

When those facts finally start to sink into my thick skull, I am able to let go of control and God proves Himself in blessing after blessing. He shows Himself to be the merciful and loving Father who wants to guide me, not through a life of misery and drudgery, but into a life of joy and hope and self-discovery. In other words, Jesus said, "If anyone would come after Me, let him deny himself and take up his cross daily and follow Me. For whoever would save his life will lose it, but whoever loses his life for My sake will save it. For what does it profit a man if he gains the whole world and loses or forfeits himself?" (Luke 9:23–25).

Sometimes sacrifice involves giving up the plans we have laid out for our lives. Some may be asked to give up corporate success in order to spend more time with their family. Others may need to sacrifice free time to care for an ailing loved one.

Not all sacrifices are large. Perhaps God wants me to give up a favorite television show that has recently become R-rated or to forfeit some private time to listen to a neighbor who is having a bad day. Maybe God is nudging me to honor my husband and bless my marriage by not insisting on my way or to forgo some sleep so I have time to read His Word.

At times, surrender is just that: giving up. It might mean laying down expectations, hopes, or dreams. Surrender is acceptance of where God has placed me now. If my current situation is not my first choice, surrender is trusting that God knows what He is doing. If my hopes have been demolished, surrender is relying on God's goodness. If my dreams have been crushed, surrender is believing God's dreams for me are even bigger than my own.

Hanging up the field marshal uniform is never easy. Denying myself an impulse that feels comfortable is not a natural inclination. Surrendering my expectations is painful. Relinquishing my rights is even harder than giving up dark chocolate. Yet when I understand that my Commanding Officer is not a punishing drill sergeant but a gentle guide and loving Lord, I readily enlist in His boot camp. I recognize that my life is not my own; the life Christ offers in exchange is one of joy and self-discovery.

> *Dear Lord, You know it's not easy for me to deny myself. I want to be in control. But I realize that because I am Your redeemed daughter, Your love for me guarantees that You will provide what is best for me. Help me to surrender daily to Your will. For Jesus' sake. Amen.*

Day Two
Wardrobe Workout

1. According to today's reading, what does it mean to deny yourself?

   What is your reaction to going to "the funeral of your own independence" (p. 41)?

2. Read Romans 12:1–13.

   a. What kind of sacrifice does God desire (v. 1)?

b. What are the first steps in becoming that kind of sacrifice (v. 2)?

c. What are some practical ways to live a life of sacrifice (vv. 3–13)?

d. How has God recently asked you to sacrifice or surrender?

3. What key lesson did you learn today?

4. Write out our memory verse for this week: "I delight to do Your will, O my God; Your law is within my heart" (Psalm 40:8). Read a phrase, then cover it and write it. Try to recite as much of the verse as you can without looking.

Day Three
<><><><><><><><><><><><>
Let God Lead

I will instruct you and teach you in the way you should go; I will counsel you and watch over you. Do not be like the horse or the mule, which have no understanding but must be controlled by bit and bridle or they will not come to you.
Psalm 32:8–9 NIV

If I have taken off the field marshal uniform, I can't continue to act like I'm the one in charge. I must listen to my Commanding Officer's instructions and trust Him to have the whole battle plan mapped out. I must follow God's lead. Scripture is full of His assurances that He will guide me, but He cautions me not to behave like a stubborn animal.

Am I acting like an obstinate mule, wanting to go left when God wants me to move to the right? Am I like a dog on a leash, pulling hard for the fire hydrant, while my Lord is trying to guide me down the sidewalk?

God does not force us to follow Him; in fact, He will not bully us into doing things His way. He gives us His Law to teach us and guide us gently to the right path. He desires to counsel us and give us the advice we need. He points out the fact that we are not like animals, which have no understanding of their master's reasons and obey simply because they are coerced. This side of heaven, we cannot completely fathom God's will, but we can trust His love and care for us. Because of that, we can be confident in His direction and follow Him willingly.

God does not want us to wear a bit and bridle, but Jesus asks us to take up His yoke: "Take My yoke upon you, and learn from Me, for I am gentle and lowly in heart, and you will find rest for your souls. For My yoke is easy, and My burden is light" (Matthew 11:29–30). A yoke is put on an animal's shoulders for the purpose of heavy labor. It is connected to a wagon or a plow—not my idea of rest! Yet Jesus says His yoke is easy. How can that be? I picture the yoke as a double yoke, and Jesus is in it with me. That's why the burden is light. Jesus is doing all the hard work! However, what happens if I try to go left when Jesus is going to the right? It will no longer be easy. I will struggle and strain and not get very far until I change direction and go with my Lord, letting Jesus gently guide me.

I am learning to let God lead in big things and small. One area I once struggled with was the education of my children. When my daughter was about ready to enter first grade, my husband, John, came up with the idea of homeschooling. I thought, "That's easy for you to say—you won't be the one doing it!" Besides, John didn't know that I had already told God that homeschooling was something I would never do! With two young children constantly under foot, I thought it would be bliss to have a few hours a day to myself. And, to be honest, I thought homeschooling was a little strange. Yet the more I researched homeschooling, the more sense it made for our family. Did that I mean that I immediately changed my mind and said, "Let's do it!"?

No. Although I recognized the advantages of homeschooling, I wanted to try that way of life about as much as I wanted to attempt a grueling marathon run. Our daughter, Anna, was also resistant to the idea, reluctant to leave the friends she had made in her kindergarten class. Through John, God was pointing one way, but Anna and I were running in the other direction.

However, it seemed to me that God was challenging me to change my "never" to "Whatever You want, Lord." He showed me that homeschooling was not only John's idea, but also God's plan for our family. I asked the Lord to change my attitude and give Anna the desire to try school at home. I began to picture cozy times reading on the couch and math at the kitchen table. One day, when I picked Anna up from kindergarten, she said, "Mom, I think we should try homeschooling next year. Nathaniel will be so lonely if I'm gone all day." My heart melted. I said yes to God's plan, gave up my idea of control, and had the great joy and privilege of educating my children for fifteen years. It was one of the best decisions we ever made!

So, how do we let God lead? Most important, we must be willing to say, "Whatever You want, Lord." We need to spend time in God's Word to discover His ways. As He teaches us in the Bible, He asks us to follow His instructions. Step by step, He will guide us in His path. Step by step, His Holy Spirit transforms our heart and makes us willing to go wherever He directs. Step by step, God the Son does the hard work as we walk in His yoke.

> *Holy Spirit, commander of my soul, guide me in the path You have mapped out for my life. Help me to say, "Whatever You want, Lord," and mean it. In Jesus' name. Amen.*

Day Three

◇◇◇◇◇◇◇◇◇◇◇◇◇◇◇◇◇◇◇◇◇◇◇◇◇◇◇

Wardrobe Workout

1. Time for an attitude check. Mark your current position on the line below.

●──●

Whatever I want   *Whatever You*
                                                    want, Lord

What have you learned today that might make it easier for you to say, "Whatever You want, Lord"?

2. Read Exodus 15:13. Write three things you discover about God's leading. Which discovery will best help you follow God's way?

3. What key lesson did you learn today?

4. Write out this week's memory verse. Try not to peek!

Day Four

⬦⬦⬦⬦⬦⬦⬦⬦⬦⬦⬦⬦⬦⬦⬦⬦⬦⬦⬦⬦⬦⬦⬦

Desire God's Desires

I delight to do Your will, O my God; Your law is within my heart.
Psalm 40:8

Some days I can honestly agree with the psalmist when he says, "I delight to do Your will, O my God," but often you may catch me crooning, "I want to do it *my way*."

The Hebrew word for *will* in the psalm means "delight, desire, or pleasure." The psalmist is saying, "God, I desire what You desire. I want to do what delights You. I am happy to accomplish whatever brings You pleasure."

This gets me thinking, "Wait a minute! If I am only doing what someone else wants, how I am *I* going to be happy? What about what *I* want to do? Doesn't it make me less of a person, even a slave, if I am only carrying out someone else's wishes?"

Jesus didn't think so! Although He is true God and has all power to do whatever He wants, He was also true man. He willingly laid aside His own inclinations to do the will of His heavenly Father. When the people of Capernaum asked what miracles Jesus was going to do in their town, He told them, "I have come down from heaven, not to do My own will but the will of Him who sent Me" (John 6:38). We might have been tempted to do some whiz-bang miracle right then and there to demonstrate our power, but Jesus did only what His Father wanted Him to do. This did not make Him a lesser person of the Trinity. He was true God. He simply desired to accomplish His Father's wishes. The Greek word for *will* here is *thelēma*, which is also defined as "wish or purpose." Jesus kept God's Law perfectly, which pleased His Father and brought Him joy.

That wasn't always easy. In the Garden of Gethsemane, Jesus asked if there was any possible way other than the cross, but He still prayed, "Nevertheless, not as I will, but as You will" (Matthew 26:39). Jesus, true man, knew the agony that physical torture and death would cause Him, and He bore the mental and emotional anguish of the sin of all the world. Jesus also knew the trauma His followers would experience when He was taken from them. Was there another way to accomplish this important work? No, there was not. This prayer is recorded so that we would know that even

God the Son is obedient to God the Father's will. Jesus did so willingly and joyfully. For example, in Samaria, when the disciples were urging Jesus to eat something, He said, "My food is to do the will of Him who sent Me and to accomplish His work" (John 4:34). Doing what pleased His Father was fuel to Jesus.

Doing what pleases my heavenly Father will also bring me joy because I am assured that He wants only what is best for me (see Jeremiah 29:11–12). One of my favorite photos of my children from when they were small is of the two of them standing at the front door ready to go out trick-or-treating for Halloween. Anna is dressed as a little princess and is clearly excited about the prospect of getting treats. Nathaniel, however, is about ready to cry, even though I made him a Thomas the Tank Engine costume so he could dress like his favorite toy. Nathaniel was only three and this was his first experience with trick-or-treating. He did not want to go out in the crisp, cool air because he didn't know what to expect. But when he came back with a bag full of candy, he was all smiles! We urged him to try something new, not to torture him, but because we knew he would enjoy the experience and would be rewarded. Our heavenly Father also knows what will be pleasant and rewarding, even though the experience may not seem beneficial to us at first.

Now my children are grown, and I am a new grandmother. Once my little grandson began to recognize us and smile, one of our favorite family activities became Make the Baby Smile. We would do anything to see that grin turn up the corners of his cute little mouth. We would get down on the floor to tickle him, play a childish game of peek-a-boo, or sacrifice our dignity by making funny faces. It was all worth it to see him beam back at us. After a recent game of Make the Baby Smile, it struck me that an even more rewarding pursuit would be Make God Smile. Am I willing to take off my field marshal uniform and obey God's Law to put a smile on my Savior's face? Am I ready to give up my prideful sense of dignity to please the Spirit living in me? Am I prepared to do anything to fulfill my heavenly Father's purposes and plans?

As God's mind-blowing love and care for me become more of a reality in my soul, may I learn to say more often, "I delight to do Your will, O my God" (Psalm 40:8).

> *Lord Jesus, help me to be like You, desiring to do God's will, not my own. Help me to remember that Your desires for me are for my good. May I live a life that puts a smile on Your face every day. Amen.*

Day Four

◇◇◇◇◇◇◇◇◇◇◇◇◇◇◇◇◇◇◇◇◇◇◇◇

Wardrobe Workout

1. Our heavenly Father wants what is best for us. If you are a parent, think of a time when your child did not comprehend "mother knows best" but later experienced happiness in doing things your way. Or, think of a time when as a child you discovered that your parents really did know what was good for you.

How can these experiences help you to trust God's ways in your life?

2. Read Jeremiah 29:9–14. In what way are we exiles?

How do these verses move you to rely more on God's perfect will for you and less on your own plans?

3. What key lesson did you learn today?

4. Write out this week's memory verse. No peeking!

◇◇◇◇◇◇◇◇◇◇◇◇◇◇◇
Study Styles

An excellent way to understand a passage is to put it in your own words. Read Romans 8:5–6 (NIV). "Those who live according to the sinful nature have their minds set on what that nature desires; but those who live in accordance with the Spirit have their minds set on what the Spirit desires. The mind of sinful man is death, but the mind controlled by the Spirit is life and peace."

Using a dictionary and thesaurus, find definitions and synonyms for the following words (note that most words will have a long list of definitions or synonyms; choose the ones that best fit the words in this passage):

Live: _____

_____

_____

Sinful: _____

_____

_____

Nature: _____

_____

_____

Desire: _____

_____

_____

Mind: _____

_____

_____

Death: _____

_____

_____

Control: _____

_____

_____

Peace: _____

_____

_____

Now using your definitions and synonyms, write Romans 8:5–6 in terms meaningful to your life:

Day Five

◇◇◇◇◇◇◇◇◇◇◇◇◇◇◇◇◇◇◇◇◇◇◇◇◇◇◇◇◇◇◇

Quit Controlling Others

*Judge not, that you be not judged. For with the judgment you
pronounce you will be judged, and with the measure you use it
will be measured to you.*
Matthew 7:1–2

I am a "take charge" kind of person. That's what got me labeled as a field
marshal in the first place! I like to have things done my way and I orchestrate (nicer
word than *manipulate*) circumstances to make sure that happens. When I find something that works for me, I tend to think everyone else should do it that way too.

But once I take off that field marshal jacket and put on battle fatigues, I realize
that not only am I not in charge of myself but I am not even in command of others.
We all wear the same uniform; we all take our orders from our Commander-in-Chief.
Of course, God may place some of us in positions of authority, but even then it is
helpful to remember that authority is not given in order to have others do things
our way. We are to concentrate on our own spiritual journey and do all things to the
glory of God.

The apostle Peter struggled with this. After Jesus and Peter had their "Simon, do
you love Me?" discussion (John 21:15–17), Jesus told Peter that when Peter was old,
others would stretch out his hands—this was understood as a prophecy of crucifix-
ion—and lead him where he did not want to go (vv. 18–19). Then Peter saw John
walking nearby and asked Jesus, "Lord, what about this man?" and Jesus answered, "If
it is My will that he remain until I come, what is that to you? You follow Me!" (vv.
21–22). Jesus told Peter not to concern himself with the circumstances of another
disciple but to keep his eyes on Jesus, following Him. We are not to worry about
another's spiritual walk, only about our own. Oswald Chambers said, "One of the
hardest lessons to learn comes from our stubborn refusal to refrain from interfering
in other people's lives. It takes a long time to realize the danger of being an amateur
providence, that is, interfering with God's plans for others" (Chambers, November
15).

James, the brother of our Lord, put it this way: "There is only one lawgiver and
judge, He who is able to save and to destroy. But who are you to judge your neigh-

bor?" (James 4:12). When we see someone doing something we know is not the best for them, we want to tell them the "right" way to do things. Often we feel this desire because we love them and want them to avoid pain or struggle. But each of us needs to pay attention to the Holy Spirit's guidance for our own lives. Another mother once told me, "Don't be your child's Holy Spirit." When our children reach a certain age, they need to learn to rely on Scripture and to listen to God's voice inside of them. (They are unlikely to hear us anyway!) The Spirit is an excellent teacher and knows when we need each lesson. Although the goal for each of us is the same—to be like Christ—we will not all learn the lessons in the same order. One of my friends, when noticing another's weakness, would simply say, "God has not brought him to that point yet." She trusted God's timing in teaching that person and did not see it as her job to judge him or fix him.

Jesus spoke concerning judging others that "with the judgment you pronounce you will be judged" (Matthew 7:2). Do I have the courage to stand before God and say, "Okay, God, judge me just as I have judged others"? I don't think so! Try as I might, the words that come out of my mouth are not always gracious.

Jesus goes on to say:

> Why do you see the speck that is in your brother's eye, but do not notice the log that is in your own eye? Or how can you say to your brother, "Let me take the speck out of your eye," when there is the log in your own eye? You hypocrite, first take the log out of your own eye, and then you will see clearly to take the speck out of your brother's eye. (Matthew 7:3–5)

This passage tells me three things. First, it informs me I have no business worrying about someone else's faults; I should just pay attention to my own. Second, my sinful nature prevents me from seeing clearly. That plank in my eye is blocking my vision—what I see as a speck of dust in someone else's eye may be nothing to be concerned about. And third, if I am honest, I have so many planks in my eyes that trying to get rid of them all will keep me busy until Jesus comes back. This will please Lord and make me an easier person to live with!

I love this version of the Seventeenth-Century Nun's Prayer that Don shares in her book *A 10-Week Journey to Becoming a Vessel God Can Use*.

> Lord, you know better than I know myself that I am growing and will someday be old. Keep me from the fatal habit of t' must say something on every subject and on every occas'

56

me from the craving to straighten out everybody's affairs. Make me thoughtful, but not moody. Helpful, but not bossy. With my vast store of wisdom, it seems a pity not to use it all, but you know, Lord, that I want a few friends at the end. . . . Give me the ability to see good things in unexpected places and talents in unexpected people. And give me, Lord, the grace to tell them so. (Partow, p. 98)

Amen to that!

So let's hang up that field marshal uniform. Let's give up the idea that we are in charge of everyone else's affairs. Let's relinquish the right to control ourselves and give command to our Lord, who knows so much better than we do what is good and right and best.

Dear Lord, You are the Lord of my life. Help me daily to surrender my life to You. Help me not to meddle in the business of others but to concentrate on my own spiritual journey. In Your name. Amen.

Day Five

◇◇◇◇◇◇◇◇◇◇◇◇◇◇◇◇◇◇◇◇◇◇

Wardrobe Workout

1. What is your reaction to the Seventeenth-Century Nun's Prayer? What part did you most relate to?

2. Jesus told Peter concerning John, "If it is My will that he remain until I come, what is that to you? You follow Me!" (John 21:22). How does this apply to your own spiritual journey?

3. What key lesson did you learn today?

4. Write Psalm 40:8 from memory.

Meaningful Makeover

Jesus said, "If anyone would come after Me, let him deny himself and take up his cross daily and follow Me" (Luke 9:23). Is there an area of your life where you are still trying to lead and have your own way? What about career? finances? relationships? Are you now ready to let Jesus get in the driver's seat? Write a prayer surrendering that area to the Lord.

Remember to bring your uniform or power suit to your group's meeting!

WEEK THREE

WORRY—Let's Bag This Accessory!

Memory Verse

Do not be anxious about anything, but in everything by prayer and supplication with thanksgiving let your requests be made known to God. And the peace of God, which surpasses all understanding, will guard your hearts and your minds in Christ Jesus.

Philippians 4:6–7

Day One

◇◇◇◇◇◇◇◇◇◇◇◇◇◇◇◇◇◇◇◇◇◇◇◇◇◇◇◇◇

The Macramé Purse

Anxiety in a man's heart weighs him down.
Proverbs 12:25

Any fashion expert will tell you that every outfit needs the right accessories. Wearing a beautiful ball gown with sweaty tennis shoes will not do! A chiffon skirt will not look right with a wide leather belt and big brass buckle (unless you're Madonna). You wouldn't wear an elegant suit while carrying an oversized, stained backpack. So while we're discarding clothes and outfits that are unflattering, let's examine the accessories we use.

Consider worry. Do you wear it like an accessory? I think worry is like a macramé purse: it is full of knots. And it's not just an accessory that we put on one day and then store in the closet the next. Some of us carry it around day after day, throwing more and more into that knotted purse until it becomes a duffle bag we drag around, weighing us down.

Worry not only burdens us, it can affect our health. Dr. Dorothy McCoy, a psychotherapist specializing in personality and wellness issues, writes to that effect on www.pioneerthinking.com. In an article on that site, Dr. McCoy claims that worry can have adverse impact on blood pressure and cholesterol levels, increase the risk of heart attack and stroke, create muscle tension that may cause headaches and other pain, and even compromise the immune system.

Now *there's* something to worry about!

Seriously, though, if that account of what worry can do to our bodies isn't enough to make us give it up, remember that worry doesn't really help. There's an old saying: "Worry is like a rocking chair; it gives you something to do, but it doesn't get you anywhere." On the other hand, I've heard people say, "Don't tell me that worry doesn't do any good. I know better. The things I worry about don't happen." Isn't that the truth! Most of the time, what we worry about never happens, and often something totally different and unexpected occurs! But that doesn't mean that worry prevents bad experiences.

The unforeseen happened the year I toured the country with a Christian singing group. We sang at churches from the East Coast to the West Coast and traveled in a converted school bus we named Miracle White, so dubbed because it was painted white and it was a miracle it was still running! One weekend in March, we were singing at a retreat at Lake Arrowhead, in the mountains of California. We had a great time, but on our way down the mountain, we noticed a little problem with Miracle White: the brakes were on fire! We were able to borrow a couple of vans to get ourselves and our equipment to our next engagement, but the repair time forced us to cancel one engagement and drive twenty-four hours straight to get to the next concert.

We were all worried about the brakes as we drove over the mountains again. The brakes held, but while driving through the Mojave Desert in the middle of the night, we heard a loud "ker-chunk" and Miracle White suddenly stopped. There we sat in the middle of the desert. Thankfully, it was March—not August—and it was night, so it was cool. A kind driver stopped and gave Bill, our leader, a ride to the nearest town. Bill came back with a tow truck, which, by the way, had "Death Valley Towing" painted on the side. That's not a great morale booster. The next day we learned that the engine had thrown a rod and would need rebuilding! So there you have it: all that worrying about the brakes was pointless!

Of course, worrying about the engine would not have been helpful either. Worry does nothing but raise your blood pressure and stress levels. So what's the solution?

This week, we will look at the causes of worry. Are there specific thoughts that produce anxiety? Can our view of God affect the level of concern we feel in our hearts? Next, we will examine how we can exchange the heavy macramé bag of worry for lighter accessories that will not weigh us down. We will learn the following:

- to trust God's provision and focus on the things that really matter;
- to live one day at a time;
- to give our problems to God; and finally,
- to retrain our minds and experience God's peace.

It is true that "Anxiety in a man's heart weighs him down" (Proverbs 12:25), but it doesn't have to. God does not want us to live burdened, troubled lives. He is ready to take that heavy bag of concerns so we can enjoy lives filled with peace and joy.

Heavenly Father, too often I find myself carrying a heavy bag of anxiety. I thank You that You are willing to take my worries and concerns. Help me to relinquish them to Your care and live in Your joy instead. In Jesus' name. Amen.

Day One
◇◇◇◇◇◇◇◇◇◇◇◇◇◇◇◇◇◇◇◇◇◇◇◇◇◇◇
Wardrobe Workout

1. In your life, is worry more like an evening bag you carry once in a while or like the bag you carry with you every day? Explore your wardrobe and find a purse or a bag that best symbolizes the way you worry. In the space below, write about the item and why it exemplifies your worry habits. If you are doing this study in a group, bring the bag or purse to the meeting and share your thoughts.

2. Read Matthew 13:3–9, 18–23.

   a. Verse 22 tells us that "the cares of the world" can make us "unfruitful." The Greek word translated as *unfruitful* is *akarpos*. It is used figuratively and means "to have no fruit, to be sterile." If that is the definition of *unfruitful*, how would you define *fruitful*?

   b. Look again at verses 7, 22. How do "the cares of the world," or what some have called "the weeds of worry," prevent a fruitful life?

c. When have you experienced the choking effects of the weeds of worry? How were you able to escape the chokehold?

3. What key lesson did you learn today?

4. Our memory verse for this week is Philippians 4:6–7: "Do not be anxious about anything, but in everything by prayer and supplication with thanksgiving let your requests be made known to God. And the peace of God, which surpasses all understanding, will guard your hearts and your minds in Christ Jesus." To help you memorize this passage, write it out in the space below.

Day Two

◇◇◇◇◇◇◇◇◇◇◇◇◇◇◇◇◇◇◇◇◇◇◇◇◇◇◇◇

Distraction and Distrust

Therefore I tell you, do not be anxious about your life, what you will eat or what you will drink, nor about your body, what you will put on. Is not life more than food, and the body more than clothing? . . . But if God so clothes the grass of the field, which today is alive and tomorrow is thrown into the oven, will He not much more clothe you, O you of little faith?
Matthew 6:25, 30

Life is not perfect. It rarely goes according to plan. Financial problems, relationship issues, and health concerns make worry and anxiety a natural part of life, right?

Not according to Jesus. His words to us are clear: "I tell you, do not be anxious" (Matthew 6:25). How is this possible?

The first step in eliminating worry from our attitude wardrobes is to recognize the source of the problem. Jesus' Sermon on the Mount talks about two underlying causes of anxiety: distraction and distrust.

Distraction

In His Sermon on the Mount, Jesus exhorts us:

> Therefore I tell you, do not be anxious about your life, what you will eat or what you will drink, nor about your body, what you will put on. Is not life more than food, and the body more than clothing? (Matthew 6:25)

The original Greek word that Jesus used for *worry* here in Matthew is *merimnaō*, which means "to be anxious about, to have a distracting care" (Vine, p. 89). When I worry about something, it is always on my mind. Whatever I am doing, my worry returns to my thought pattern, distracting me from what is important. Too often, when anxiety and concern start to invade my mind, I let them! My macramé handbag of worry may start out small, but with each anxious thought, I add another knot.

However, God's grace and power can untangle my threads of anxiety, freeing my mind from tension and fear. The King James Version translates "Do not worry" as "Take no thought." This reminds me of a mother who sees her child about to jump into a mud puddle with his Sunday clothes on and yells, "Don't even think about it!" Jesus, in effect, is saying to me, "Don't even think about it! Don't let those troubling thoughts continue to tangle and trap your mind." Anxiety may threaten to thread its way into my thoughts, but in God's power, I can resist the temptation to grasp its cords and permanently bind them to my mind. The Holy Spirit will help me to fasten my thoughts on God's grace while He untangles my problems.

Jesus continues to talk about distractions in His famous sermon:

> Look at the birds of the air: they neither sow nor reap nor gather into barns, and yet your heavenly Father feeds them. Are you not of more value than they? And which of you by being anxious can add a single hour to his span of life? And why are you anxious about clothing? Consider the lilies of the field, how they grow: they neither toil nor spin, yet I tell you, even Solomon in all his glory was not arrayed like one of these. (Matthew 6:26–29)

Jesus urges me not to be distracted with the material cares of life. He reminds me that there are more important things than satisfying physical needs and looking good! God gives food to tiny birds and stunning garments to fleeting flowers; He promises to provide for me as well. Living in America, I have never been too concerned about getting enough to eat, but when I worry, it is often about the physical stuff of life: "Will we have enough money to pay all the bills? Will the roof on the house hold out for one more year? How will we pay for the kids' college education?" I may not worry about having enough clothes, but I may worry about having the right clothes. My kids may bug me for a certain brand of tennis shoes or I might see a designer bag I think I must have. God invites me to concentrate on His goodness and provision instead of what television commercials declare I need.

I have to admit that not long ago, I was seriously distracted by the issue of clothing. While helping my daughter plan her wedding, one of my tasks was to find a mother-of-the-bride dress. I hunted through store after store and tried on dozens of dresses, but I couldn't find anything just right. This one was too fancy; that one was too plain. Many revealed too much on top, while others amplified my backside (not a pretty sight). One made me look like an upside-down tulip! At one point, I even purchased four different dresses, trying to narrow down the possibilities. This fashion crisis started to invade my thoughts as I envisioned the perfect dress and wondered where else I could look. I told myself it was silly. No one was even going to notice me at the wedding! Yet my mind persisted in this distraction. Finally, I remembered Jesus' words, "Why are you anxious about clothing?" (v. 28), and I gave my anxiety over to Him. (I ended up returning three of the previously purchased dresses and altering the fourth. It looked great! So why did I worry?)

Distrust

Jesus opened this section of His Sermon on the Mount by asking, "Why are you anxious?" He concludes with another question:

> But if God so clothes the grass of the field, which today is alive and tomorrow is thrown into the oven, will He not much more clothe you, O you of little faith? (Matthew 6:30)

Here, Jesus equates worry with faithlessness. Lack of trust in God's care is a second underlying cause of anxiety. Little faith equals big worries.

Is my faith so small because I make God small? My human mind sometimes attempts to craft God in my image. I limit His goodness and power because I subconsciously picture Him to be like me: powerless, selfish, and unwilling to help. Yet God assures me that He is in control of the situation and that He wants what is best for me. He delights in holding my hand as I go through life.

Next, Jesus teaches me:

> Therefore do not be anxious, saying, "What shall we eat?" or "What shall we drink?" or "What shall we wear?" For the Gentiles seek after all these things, and your heavenly Father knows that you need them all. (Matthew 6:31–32)

The Greek verb tense for "Do not be anxious" is present imperative: it's a command. Jesus doesn't say, "I *suggest* you don't spend your time worrying," or "You know, worrying is not really a great idea." He comes right out with the order, "Don't worry." When I dwell on my concerns, I disobey Christ's instructions. Worry is sin.

In addition, I believe Christ's statement, "Do not be anxious," is also an invitation, an offer to carry my macramé bag of concerns and apprehensions. Unbelievers, those who do not trust in the one true God, do not have this option. Jesus tells me to exhibit to the world that I have a loving Father who takes care of all my needs instead of acting like someone who does not have God as my strength.

Distraction and distrust. Are these present in your life? Are they contributing to your anxiety? Jesus requests that we not let distracting thoughts entangle our minds. Instead, He wants us to allow Him to loosen our knotted problems. He invites us to exchange distrust for confidence in the goodness and unlimited resources of our caring Father.

*Heavenly Father, forgive me when I have allowed distraction
and distrust to entangle my mind. Help me to fasten my thoughts
on Your promise of provision. I give You my handbag of worries,
trusting that You know what is best for me. In Jesus' name. Amen.*

Day Two
Wardrobe Workout

1. According to today's reading, what are two causes of worry? Which one most often leads you to anxiety?

2. God wants us to exchange our distrust for confidence in His goodness and strength. Read the following passages and discover special promises for those who trust the Lord.

Psalm 9:10 _____

_____

Psalm 32:10 _____

_____

Psalm 56:3–4 _____

_____

Psalm 91:14 _____

_____

3. What key lesson did you learn today?

4. Write out our memory verse for this week: "Do not be anxious about anything, but in everything by prayer and supplication with thanksgiving let your
   requests be made known to God. And the peace of God, which surpasses all
   understanding, will guard your hearts and your minds in Christ Jesus" (Philippians 4:6–7). Write it out phrase by phrase, trying to do as much of it as you
   can from memory.

Day Three

◇◇◇

New Accessories: Trusting and Seeking

For the Gentiles seek after all these things,
and your heavenly Father knows that you need them all.
But seek first the kingdom of God and His righteousness,
and all these things will be added to you.
Matthew 6:32–33

Handbags come in many shapes and styles. Clutch purses, satchel purses, and backpack purses. Leather bags, quilted bags, and animal-print bags. I've seen brown bags, black bags, and pink-and-lime-green bags. Women carry purses with ruffles or fringe, rhinestones or bows. One young woman I know carries a purse shaped like an electric guitar!

Purses also vary in size. I prefer a medium-sized bag to hold my wallet, hairbrush, and planner. My friend Deb, however, uses a minuscule pink bag just large enough for her cell phone, a couple of credit cards, and a bit of cash. On the other end of the spectrum is our friend Sophie, who carries a ten-pound tote every day. We often tease her about this suitcase, but guess to whom we turn when we need a bandage, toothpick, sewing kit, tape measure, hand sanitizer, cough drop, aspirin, or antacid?

In my spiritual life, I have often tried to carry a Sophie-sized bag stuffed with worries and concerns. Each time another problem came along, I stuffed it in my knotted macramé bag and dragged it with me everywhere. Distraction and distrust weighed me down and prevented me from realizing that better accessories were available.

God's Word reminds me that Jesus has offered to take my anxiety and concern. As He gently slides that bag of worries from my shoulder, He offers me fresh, new accessories: His love and provision and His kingdom and righteousness.

Trusting in God's Love and Provision

Jesus encourages me to carry a new handbag: a renewed reliance in God's care for me. Jesus told the crowd on the mountain, "Your heavenly Father knows that you need them all" (Matthew 6:32). Before I voice my concern, before I yearn for something more, before I can even conceive a new desire, my Father knows what I long for and what I require. Do I really believe this, or am I still thinking that I know what I need and want better than my Maker and Designer?

One of the wise women in my Bible study group said that when her grown children would ask her what she wanted for her birthday or for Christmas, she used to give a detailed request. But when she received exactly what she had asked for, she soon discovered that she didn't really like it after all. She began to tell her children, "You pick something out. You do a much better job of choosing something for me." And she found the gifts much more to her liking! Can I come to that point with God and trust Him to give me something better than I had even considered, something that is infinitely more satisfying than what I thought I wanted? Jesus is trying to tell me that my heavenly Father wants to clothe me with a wardrobe more beautiful than a king's. He wants to shower me with gifts beyond my imagination! He wants to take my burdens on Himself and give me peace and joy in exchange.

In faith—a gift of the Holy Spirit—I can believe and trust that my heavenly Father knows exactly what I need and provides for me, both in my earthly life and for my eternal life.

Seek God's Kingdom and His Righteousness

The next accessory Jesus instructs us to carry at all times is a new mind-set. Jesus continues, "But seek first the kingdom of God and His righteousness, and all these things will be added to you" (Matthew 6:33).

This is the second step in leaving worry behind: be concerned with God's kingdom and God's righteousness.

What is God's kingdom? Jesus said, "My kingdom is not of this world" (John 18:36), and the Book of Daniel tells us, "His kingdom is an everlasting kingdom" (Daniel 4:3). To explain further what is eternal, Paul writes, "We look not to the things that are seen but to the things that are unseen. For the things that are seen are transient, but the things that are unseen are eternal" (2 Corinthians 4:18). When I fixate on the size of my house or my television or on whether hemlines are up or down this year, I've got it all wrong—I've fallen for Satan's subtle temptations. Material things will not last for eternity. What will endure forever? The things we can't see, such as faith, hope, love, peace, and joy. What never goes out of style? Character traits such as humility, patience, and self-control. God's love and His Word will endure forever (Psalm 136).

When I concentrate on these things, I use my time well, because they will be here now and in eternity. When I am more attentive to how much my faith has developed over the last year instead of how much my bank account has grown, then my thoughts are attuned to the eternal rather than the temporal. When I am more absorbed in developing my patience, not my purse collection, then I am pursuing something of everlasting value.

The other item that Jesus directs me to seek is God's righteousness. Because Jesus took the punishment for my sins, I can stand pure and holy before God. Because the Holy Spirit gave me the gift of faith when I was baptized, I have received the robe of righteousness. As my faith life develops, I grow into that robe. As I live righteously, my life will appear more like God sees me—pure and unstained. The Spirit will help me refashion my actions to match the character of Jesus.

I ask myself, "Am I using this new mind-set as my favorite accessory or am I still clinging to the purse of worldly worries?" As I change my focus to concentrate on these two things—seeking God's rule in my heart and the refashioning of my character—other concerns will fall away as unimportant. Christ will shoulder my bag of worries.

Let's abandon any ten-pound bags of worry or anxiety we may be carrying and take up the new accessories of trusting God's love and seeking His will in our lives.

Dearest Jesus, too often I carry a heavy tote of worry and anxiety. Thank You for taking that heavy bag from me. Help me to grow in my trust in Your love. Refashion my spirit to seek what is eternal. Amen.

Day Three
Wardrobe Workout

1. Most often, when concerns and cares try to crowd my mind:

   _____ I confidently trust God to handle my problems.

   _____ I try to fix them myself, because I don't trust God.

   _____ I try to fix my problems myself, because I think I can do a better job.

_____ I try to fix my problems myself, because I'm not sure God will fix things to my liking.

Why did you answer the way you did?

2. When we learn to use new accessories such as trusting God's love and seeking His kingdom, we will experience peace instead of anxiety. Read John 16:33.

a. What does Jesus want us to have? What is Jesus' peace like?

b. Sometimes when we encounter problems we question, "Why me?" But what does Jesus tell us we can expect in this world? How does this help us answer the question, "Why me?"

c. Jesus said, "Take heart, I have overcome the world." According to that statement, which of these sentences is true?

_____ Jesus will conquer the world in the future.

_____ Jesus is in the process of conquering the world and its problems.

_____ Jesus has already conquered the world and its problems.

How does this help you have peace in the midst of your current troubles?

3. What key lesson did you learn today?

4. Write out this week's memory verse. Try not to peek.

Day Four

 ⬦⬦⬦⬦⬦⬦⬦⬦⬦⬦⬦⬦⬦⬦⬦⬦⬦⬦⬦⬦⬦⬦⬦⬦⬦⬦⬦⬦⬦⬦⬦⬦⬦⬦⬦

New Accessories: Living and Giving

*Therefore do not worry about tomorrow, for tomorrow will worry
about itself. Each day has enough trouble of its own.*
Matthew 6:34 NIV

You have probably heard the idiom, "You can't make a silk purse out of a sow's ear." It is also true that you can't make a purse of peace out of a handbag of worry. However, God's Word offers us two accessories that can bring serenity: living one day at a time and giving our problems to God.

Live One Day at a Time

In His Sermon on the Mount, Jesus describes one more way to eliminate worry: "Therefore do not worry about tomorrow. . . . Each day has enough trouble of its own" (Matthew 6:34). In other words, live one day at a time. Sometimes I think of it this way: if my life is a novel, I am to concern myself with the page I am on, and not on all the twists and turns the plot may take later in the book. In a way, this should be easy, since I know how the story concludes. Because Jesus is my Savior, I know my happy ending is guaranteed! I will be with Him in heaven. Therefore, I am free to concentrate on life here and now, on *this* page. I can make plans, but I need to realize that God is in control of the universe and circumstances may change along the way.

In his book *How to Stop Worrying and Start Living* (Simon & Schuster, 1984), Dale Carnegie recounts what Sir William Osler told a group of students at Yale in 1913. Osler encouraged them to cultivate the habit of a life of "day-tight compartments." He urged these students to stop dwelling in the past and worrying about the future and, instead, to live fully in the present. Osler explained that living in the past or the future creates burdens too heavy for even the strongest to bear (Carnegie, p. 24). Doesn't that sound familiar? Jesus said, "Each day has enough trouble of its own." It does no good to spend our energy on things we cannot change about the past or to get anxious about things that might happen in the future. Anxiety about those things is wasted energy. Instead, we are guided to do what we can today and to do it with enthusiasm and the strength God gives us to complete our tasks. Fashion your mind to live one day at a time and your load will be lighter!

Give Your Problems to God

The apostle Paul also talks about worry in his letter to the Philippians:

> Do not be anxious about anything, but in everything by prayer and supplication with thanksgiving let your requests be made known to God. And the peace of God, which surpasses all understanding, will guard your hearts and your minds in Christ Jesus. (Philippians 4:6–7)

When I persist in worrying, allowing anxious thoughts to continue, I constantly carry my macramé bag. I tote that purse made of knots and entanglements wherever I go. It's becoming heavier and heavier! What can I do to rid myself of that burdensome bag of anxiety? When I trust God, I can give it to Him! The word *anxious* that Paul uses here is that same *merimnaō* Jesus used in Matthew, meaning "distracted." Don't be distracted by worrisome thoughts. Instead, when they pop up, transfer them back to God in prayer. Our loving Father says we can bring anything and everything to Him. Nothing is too big or too small.

Sometimes I insist on carrying my problems myself. (Did I mention that I can be stubborn?) Perhaps I'm reluctant to admit that I can't solve my troubles on my own. So I tote that bag, trying to find a comfortable position for it. I shift it from one sore shoulder to the other. I stare at the knots, hoping to find a way to untangle the situation. Finally, when I have tried everything I can think of, I throw up my hands in helplessness and scream, "I can't do it anymore!" Jesus smiles (trying not to laugh at my pigheadedness) and gladly takes the tangled mess from my hands.

If I am honest, I am reluctant to let go of my problems because I'm not sure God will fix them to my liking! Satan encourages me to believe that giving the problems to God is like giving control to a mean ogre. I need to remind myself that God does not want me to give Him my bag of worries just so He can make my life miserable. He loves me passionately and cares for me affectionately. Life is not always easy. In fact, Jesus tells us that "you will weep and lament. . . . You will be sorrowful" (John 16:20). But immediately, our loving Lord promises that He has our best interests in mind: "Your sorrow will turn into joy" (v. 20) So I ask myself, "Do I really believe that God loves me? Do I trust that He will handle my problems in a way that is best for me?"

Why doesn't God automatically take my knotted handbag when He sees me struggling with it? Although our Lord has the power to act as tyrant, He doesn't. He wants me to offer up my life willingly, to give Him my problems because I trust in His goodness and love, to experience His unlimited power and resources as I place each crisis in His hands, and to experience the ultimate relief when I cease to struggle. As I learn to release, I can get a glimpse of how big God is compared to my problems.

Henry Ford is quoted as saying, "I believe God is managing affairs and that He doesn't need any advice from me. With God in charge, I believe everything will work out for the best in the end. So what is there to worry about?"

Almighty God, too often I have been anxious about the future. Help me to live one day at a time. Many times I have stubbornly held on to my problems, thinking I can solve them on my own. Help me to trust Your power to work everything for the best. In Jesus' name and for His sake. Amen.

Day Four

◇◇◇◇◇◇◇◇◇◇◇◇◇◇◇◇◇◇◇◇◇◇◇◇◇◇◇◇

Wardrobe Workout

1. Instead of carrying our worries, Peter instructs us to "Cast all your anxiety on Him because He cares for you" (1 Peter 5:7 NIV). The Greek word for *care* is *melei* and means "to care for or be concerned about." How does this knowledge of God's care help you to give Him your troubles?

2. Luther's Small Catechism explains the First Commandment this way: "We should fear, love, and trust in God above all things." Look up the following verses and comment on trusting God.

Psalm 73:25–26 _____

_____

Psalm 118:8 _____

_____

Proverbs 3:5 _____

_____

1 Samuel 17:37, 46–47 _____

_____

Matthew 10:28 _____

_____

3. What key lesson did you learn today?

4. Write this week's memory verse.

◇◇◇◇◇◇◇◇◇◇◇◇◇
Study Styles

We have been talking about God's peace in our lives. One way to study the Bible is to look for PEACE: a **P**romise, an **E**xample to follow (or not follow), an **A**ttitude to cultivate, a **C**ommand to obey, and an **E**nlargement of my view of God.

Here is an example from John 14:

Promise: "Peace I leave with you; My peace I give you" (v. 27).

Example: "Thomas said to Him, 'Lord, we do not know where You are going. How can we know the way?' " (v. 5). We can follow Thomas's example in asking questions.

Attitude: "Whoever has My commandments and keeps them, he it is who loves Me" (v. 21). Attitude of obedience in love.

Command: "Let not your hearts be troubled. Believe in God; believe also in Me" (v. 1).

Enlargement: "But the Helper, the Holy Spirit, whom the Father will send in My name, He will teach you all things and bring to your remembrance all that I have said to you" (v. 26).

Now it's your turn. Find PEACE in Isaiah 26.

Promise: _____

_____

Example: _____

_____

Attitude: _____

_____

Command: _____

_____

Enlargement: _____

_____

Day Five

◇◇◇◇◇◇◇◇◇◇◇◇◇◇◇◇◇◇◇◇◇◇◇

Retrain Your Mind

*Finally, brothers, whatever is true, whatever is honorable, whatever
is just, whatever is pure, whatever is lovely, whatever is commendable,
if there is any excellence, if there is anything worthy of praise,
think about these things.*
Philippians 4:8

On a few occasions (okay, more than a few), I have given my handbag of worries to God and said, "Here, please carry this for me," only to wrestle it out of His hands again the next day, the next hour, sometimes the next minute! My shoulder and back start aching again under the heavy load (sometimes literally) and I wonder why I feel so burdened. Then I recognize that bag of tricks hanging on my shoulder again, and sheepishly I hand it over to the One who has been trying to hold it all along. Hopefully, as I progress in my journey with the Lord, I become swifter in giving my problems back to God.

Perhaps you have noticed this problem in your own life. How can we learn to let God carry our bag of worries for good? I believe the solution is to retrain our minds. In Philippians 4:8, Paul advises us to think about what is true. We might define this as those things we know without doubt are real, verifiable, and quantifiable. Don't think about what *might* come true. Don't sugar-coat the situation, but don't make it worse than it is. When I have a sticky problem, I sometimes let my mind take me beyond the current difficulty and speculate where the predicament might lead. My mind may even exaggerate the problem. Think about what is honorable. Dwell on what is just and pure, what is lovely or dear to you, and what you admire and respect. Meditate on what is excellent, perfect, and good. Fix your thoughts on things that are praiseworthy: things that deserve applause or commendation.

As I am writing this, God is giving me an opportunity to put these words into practice. Next week, my daughter and her husband are going overseas. For eleven months. Or longer. Perhaps for thirty years. And they have the audacity to want to take my grandson with them! My son-in-law is taking a short-term position as an

English teacher in a faraway country, but their hope is to lead the people in a darkened land to the light of Christ.

Although I am pleased that they want to serve our Lord and Savior, I admit that my primary emotion is worry. I am concerned for their safety, afraid their travel will be difficult and dangerous, and nervous about their well-being in a foreign culture. Perhaps most of all, I am apprehensive that I will spend each day trying to hold back tears (and be unsuccessful) as my arms ache for the hugs that are not possible.

My loving Savior reminds me that the key to ending this cycle of anxiety is to retrain my mind. Instead of continuing to tote my bag of worry, I am trying to concentrate on what is true: God is in control and He will take care of my daughter and her young family. I will strive to think about what is right and excellent: it is right that they are seeking to follow God's will. I will reflect on what is pure, their desire to serve God, and what I admire: their dedication! (Maybe I will also offer to babysit my grandson for a little while—say, eleven months?)

After I have given my macramé bag of worry to the good will of God, I can become more consistent in using my new accessories: trusting in God's provision, seeking His kingdom, living one day at a time, giving my problems to God, and retraining my mind. As these new fashions become my way of life, I can experience God's peace.

How can God's peace change our lives? Paul told the Philippians that "the peace of God, which surpasses all understanding, will guard your hearts and your minds in Christ Jesus" (Philippians 4:7). That word *guard* is *phroureō* in the Greek language. It is a military term, meaning "to keep under guard, to provide protection." It is used in "the sense of that security that is his when [the Christian] puts all his matters into the hand of God" (Vine, p. 284). How wonderful! Once I have given God all my anxieties and perplexing worries, His peace will be like a military guard, providing protection and blocking out all of my enemies—even worry. I am secure and calm when I let God take my apprehensions.

Jesus instructed His disciples about the peace He freely gives: "Peace I leave with you; My peace I give to you. I do not give to you as the world gives. Do not let your hearts be troubled and do not be afraid" (John 14:27 NIV). Jesus left His peace here with us. What was Jesus' peace like? In the Gospels, we see that although Jesus' days were packed with activity, He never seemed stressed. Even when other people around Him were anxious, Jesus was calm. Mark 4:35–41 tells about the time when Jesus and the disciples were sailing on the Sea of Galilee and a storm blew up. The possibility of drowning was real. The disciples were frantic, but Jesus was asleep in the back of the boat. You can't get much more relaxed than that! Not only was Jesus calm, but He also then calmed the storm (Mark 4:39). My mind may argue, "Of course Jesus could be calm. He is God! He is in control of the universe. What did He have to be afraid of?" But Jesus said, "My peace I give you." This same peace is mine when I remember that He is in charge.

Jesus says, "Do not let your hearts be troubled" (John 14:27 NIV). We don't *have* to stay in a state of agitation and fear. It's natural to shop in the mall of anxiety, but we don't have to linger there. When fear and doubt rise in our hearts, we need to go to Jesus, give Him our problems, and exchange them for His tranquility and serenity, His quietness and comfort. Then we can experience His peace: the kind of peace that lets us sleep through a raging storm while we are riding in a twelve-foot dinghy!

Look at your shoulder. Is that heavy bag of knots still hanging there? If so, throw it off!

> *Lord Jesus, help me to think on what is true, honorable, just, and pure. Retrain my mind to dwell on what is lovely, excellent, and worthy of praise. Thank You for Your peace, which guards my mind against worry, fear, and doubt. Amen.*

Day Five
◇◇◇◇◇◇◇◇◇◇◇◇◇◇◇◇◇◇◇◇◇◇
Wardrobe Workout

1. Which of these new accessories do you find most useful?

   _____ Trusting God's love and provision.

   _____ Seeking God's kingdom and righteousness.

   _____ Living one day at a time.

   _____ Giving my problems to God.

   _____ Retraining my mind.

   Think of a practical way to use these accessories this week. Write it here.

2. Read Psalm 25 and Hebrews 2:5–13. How do these passages comfort you?

3. What key lesson did you learn today?

4. Write out Philippians 4:6–7, our memory verse for this week. No peeking!

Meaningful Makeover

Choose one problem that is occupying your mind right now. See if you can apply Philippians 4:8 (NIV) to this situation. What about this problem is:

True: _____

_____

Noble: _____

_____

Right: _____

_____

Pure: _____

_____

Lovely: _____

_____

Admirable: _____

_____

Excellent: _____

_____

Praiseworthy: _____

_____

(If you cannot find some of these qualities in that particular situation, find them in other areas of your life.)

Remember to bring your purse or bag to your group's meeting!

WEEK FOUR

PRIDE—Purge the Prom Dress

Memory Verse

Clothe yourselves, all of you, with humility toward one another, for "God opposes the proud but gives grace to the humble."

1 Peter 5:5

Day One

◇◇◇◇◇◇◇◇◇◇◇◇◇◇◇◇◇◇◇◇◇◇◇◇◇◇◇◇◇◇

The Prom Dress of Pride

Pride goes before destruction, and a haughty spirit before a fall.
Proverbs 16:18

Would you believe I still have a high school prom dress in my closet? I do! After all, you never can tell when you might need a formal gown that was in style, say, thirty years ago, right? This particular dress is made of white eyelet fabric—yards and yards of white eyelet fabric. The neckline is accented with a gathered capelet of the pure white material that skims the shoulders and ends just above the elbows. The fitted waistline is adorned with two six-foot long sashes that wrap around the waist and tie in a humongous bow in the back. From the waist flows a very full skirt trimmed with a ten-inch ruffle of more of the wonderful eyelet! This stunning dress is like pride: it's an attention-getter to be sure, but the skirt is so big that it doesn't let people get close, and it often trips me up. I've been meaning to purge both the prom dress and pride from my closet, but haven't been successful.

Back in sixth grade, I had another outfit that tripped me up and led me to experience that old adage, "Pride goes before a fall." Everyone in my class was learning to play the recorder, and we were getting pretty good. I had an edge, however: I had studied piano since kindergarten, so I knew how to read music. I attended a school associated with a church, and one day our teacher announced that our class was going to sing for one of the evening services and that three members of our class would also be playing the recorder. Well, didn't I think I was something when I was chosen to be one of the three! That night, I was ready to burst my buttons. Not only was I going to be one of the three recorder players, but also, my mother had just given me my first pair of real panty hose, and I was going to wear them that night!

Upon arriving at the church, I climbed the long, dark staircase to the balcony to join my classmates. With each step, the music of the organ grew louder. When I reached the top of the stairs, I stood for a moment at the back of the balcony, looking down the short aisle leading to the front of the balcony. The organ was directly in front of me, and I knew Mr. Giese was at the keyboard of the great instrument, although I couldn't see him behind his sheet music. My classmates were already sitting in the rich wooden pews on either side of the aisle. As I walked down the four or five carpeted steps to the front of the balcony where the recorder players were to stand, I tripped and landed flat on my bottom with a deafening thud! I looked down at my legs. My new panty hose were no longer beautiful. Huge holes exposed my knees, and dozens of runners sprinted up and down my legs. The organ music was now accompanied by the stifled laughter of my classmates. While still playing, Mr. Giese somehow managed to raise himself up so he could peer over his sheet music to see what had made the sudden noise. To top off the evening, I overheard some conversations while waiting for my mother in the entryway after the service (as I was trying to hide behind a pillar to obscure the view of my panty hose). One man questioned his wife, "Do you know what made that sonic boom before the service began?" It was not my finest moment.

While that encounter with pride led to a literal fall, there have been many times since then that my smugness resulted in humiliating failure. What is it about pride that trips me up? I think it may cause me to fall because I'm looking down at other people rather than watching where I am going. I'm too busy looking at myself to notice the pitfalls around me. I'm too worried about how I look in my prom dress to realize it is only causing me to stumble.

To avoid tripping over my prom dress of pride, I need to be willing to part with superiority and conceit. I need to step out of the limelight and quit craving attention. My attitudes of arrogance and haughtiness need to be thrown out.

Instead, I will change into the clothing of humility. This garment turns attention to others, takes an interest in their concerns, and serves them without expecting anything in return. Most important, humility puts God above all, even above myself.

No matter how long we have been keeping that prom dress in our closets, let's get rid of pride and arrogance. Let's learn to wear humility.

Heavenly Father, although I don't like to admit it, sometimes I still wear my old prom dress of pride. At times, I look down on others because of their social or economic position. On occasion, I find myself so busy looking at myself that I don't notice the people around me. Help me to change; help me to wear the clothing of humility. In Jesus' name. Amen.

Day One
◇◇◇◇◇◇◇◇◇◇◇◇◇◇◇◇◇◇◇◇◇◇◇◇◇
Wardrobe Workout

1. Do you still have a prom dress in your closet? If so, dig it out! If not, try to find a photo of yourself in a formal dress. Bring the dress or photo to your group meeting. Try to recall your emotions the day you wore the dress or when the photo was taken. Were they prideful feelings? Why or why not?

2. Read the following verses and record the results of pride.

   a. Proverbs 11:2 _____

   _____

   b. Proverbs 29:23 _____

   _____

   c. Isaiah 2:17 _____

   _____

   Have you personally experienced that "pride goes before a fall"? If you want, share a real-life incident. Remember that after a little time has passed, our most embarrassing events often become our funniest stories!

How do your own experiences reflect the message of the above verses?

3. What key lesson did you learn today?

4. Our memory verse for this week is 1 Peter 5:5: "Clothe yourselves, all of you, with humility toward one another, for 'God opposes the proud but gives grace to the humble.'" To help you memorize this verse, write it out in the space below.

Day Two
⬦⬦⬦⬦⬦⬦⬦⬦⬦⬦⬦⬦⬦⬦⬦⬦⬦⬦⬦⬦⬦⬦⬦⬦⬦⬦⬦
Prideful Prom Dress Style

The teachers of the law and the Pharisees sit in Moses' seat. So you
must obey them and do everything they tell you. But do not do
what they do, for they do not practice what they preach. . . .
Everything they do is done for men to see.
Matthew 23:2–3, 5 (NIV)

The prom dress of pride. In today's culture of vanity, this high-fashion attitude wins awards and is praised by critics. Important people pursue even more important positions. Famous people chase after even more fame. Reality TV makes it seem as though everyone is trying to capture the world's attention.

You might be wondering, "Excessive pride is an unattractive trait, but is all pride bad? Is it wrong to have a little satisfaction in turning out a respectable loaf of whole-wheat bread after six previous tries yielded only inedible bricks? Is it sinful to beam at the sight of your six-year-old reciting his lines perfectly in the school play? Is it wicked to show the confidence you have because of forgiveness in Christ?"

No. Taking pleasure in a job well done and delighting in a loved one's successes is not the same as pride. Nor does Jesus want us to mope around looking like miserable failures when He has freed us from sin and eternal death.

However, the prom dress of pride is different from delight or joy. Pride is fashioned with layers and layers of self-importance, attention-getting ruffles, a hoopskirt of superiority, and a corset of conceit. Arrogant lacy details of lofty airs complete the look.

Remember how Cinderella could not go to the ball without her ball gown? Conversely, you and I cannot fully enter a celebration of God's grace while we wear that ball gown of pride. All those tiers of arrogance and self-satisfaction prevent us from fitting through the door of God's mercy. When I am wearing that full-length gown of smugness, I may not even realize I need God's compassion. I may not understand my desperate need of forgiveness.

Let's examine the prom dress of pride more closely. How is it put together?

The first details I notice are the attention-getting ruffles! My old prom dress and the gown of arrogance share this fashion feature. The clothing of conceit is always worn to catch someone's eye. The prideful prom-goer wears ruffles of attention, hoping that all the people will turn their heads and murmur, "Who is that?"

Jesus often held up the Pharisees as bad examples when He taught His disciples. Because the Pharisees were the religious leaders in authority, Jesus instructed His disciples to obey them (see Luther's explanation of the Fourth Commandment in the Small Catechism). But in Mark 7, Jesus cautioned His followers about very specific examples of behaviors that were evident among the Pharisees and nonbelievers. Note that He calls these behaviors "evil":

> [Jesus] said, "What comes out of a person is what defiles him. For from within, out of the heart of man, come evil thoughts, sexual immorality, theft, murder, adultery, coveting, wickedness, deceit, sensuality, envy, slander, pride, foolishness. All these evil things come from within, and they defile a person." (Mark 7:20–23)

Christ directed His friends never to imitate such behavior, for "everything they do is done for men to see" (Matthew 23:5 NIV). The Pharisees wanted attention, praise, and admiration. They desired the approval of men and titles of honor.

If I am honest, I, too, have acted like a Pharisee. I have taken on tasks simply because I know they are high profile. Perhaps then people will notice me, pat me on the back, and maybe even put my name in the church bulletin!

Instead, Jesus encourages working behind the scenes, taking the dirty jobs, and serving without commendation. He told His disciples, "The greatest among you shall be your servant" (Matthew 23:11). Let's not emulate those Pharisees who did everything for the praise and attention of men. Jesus applauds those who are willing to be overlooked, and His applause should be our goal. When the rest of the world tries to attract attention and obtain the world's approval, we can be content to stay in the background and receive a standing ovation from the only One who really matters. As we lose the prom dress of pride, we are ready for the Holy Spirit's miraculous touch. He can transform our self-importance into humbleness.

Instead of that head-turning dress with ruffles of attention, let's select willingness to go unnoticed as our clothing of choice. Humility is the garment we require to realize our need for the gift of God's compassion. When I see myself not as an important person but simply as a treasured child, I am drawn closer to my magnificent Lord and Savior. Without the gown of arrogance, I can attend a gala of grace and celebrate God's love and forgiveness.

Holy Spirit, I am ready for Your miraculous touch. Transform my need for attention into the willingness to go unnoticed. Although everyone else clamors for the world's attention, help me live for the applause of just one: my Savior, Jesus. Amen.

Day Two
◇◇◇◇◇◇◇◇◇◇◇◇◇◇◇◇◇◇◇◇◇◇◇◇
Wardrobe Workout

1. Discuss the aspects of pride. For example, what differences do you see between arrogance and dignity?

2. King Uzziah, one of the faithful kings of the kingdom of Judah, experienced a downfall because of his pride. The life of this lesser-known king demonstrates that even the faithful struggle with this sin. Read 2 Chronicles 26.

   a. What do verses 1–5 tell you about Uzziah's early life? How can you tell he was faithful?

b. Verses 6–15 list some of the good things that King Uzziah did for his king-dom. Summarize them. Why was he so successful (v. 15)?

c. Verses 16–20 detail his descent from royal rule. What led to his downfall (v. 16)? Through what act did Uzziah's pride manifest itself? Why was this wrong (v. 18)? Why do you think pride propelled him to that action?

d. The end of Uzziah's life is recounted in verses 21–23. How would you de-scribe the eulogies at his funeral (v. 23)? How do you think they might have been different if his pride had not gotten him into trouble (for example, v. 4)?

3. What key lesson did you learn today?

4. Write out our memory verse for this week: "Clothe yourselves, all of you, with humility toward one another, for 'God opposes the proud but gives grace to the humble'" (1 Peter 5:5). Write it out phrase by phrase, trying to do as much of it as you can from memory.

Day Three

◇◇◇

The Hoopskirt of Superiority and the Corset of Conceit

For everyone who exalts himself will be humbled,
but the one who humbles himself will be exalted.
Luke 18:14

Are you ready to throw out your prom dress of pride? Do you want to gather up all those tiers of arrogance and attention-getting ruffles and toss them into God's recycle bin? While you're at it, don't forget the underpinnings: the hoopskirt of superiority and the corset of conceit.

You see, when I'm wearing all those layers of self-importance, I am certain to put on my hoopskirt of superiority to make them stand out. I pull that gown of pride out of my closet in hopes that others will notice my significance, value, and worth. Wishing to appear more important than others, I am tempted to don that old dress of arrogance.

The Pharisees provided Jesus with another teaching opportunity when they exhibited their desire for superiority. In his Gospel, Luke tells the story of Jesus and His disciples eating at the home of a prominent Pharisee (Luke 14:7–11). Jesus noticed that all the guests were jockeying for the best places at the table. They all wanted the seats of honor. But the wise Teacher instructed His friends that this was a foolish practice. After all, He said, someone may choose a good seat, sit down, and start chatting with his neighbors when someone more important comes in. The host will ask the first guest to move further down the table to make room for this distinguished guest. Rather than suffer the embarrassment pride can cause, Jesus advised His hearers to take the lowest place instead. Then, when the host sees the humble guest, he will insist that the guest move up, and he will be honored in front of everyone. In other words, don't assume that you are better than others or that you should have the seat of honor.

This is no different from society today. The fastest person wins the race, the most talented actor gets the role, and the graduate with the most impressive résumé obtains the job. Therefore, I want to be the best, the fastest, and the most impressive. I may shove others to the back of the line so I can get ahead. But the Bible encourages us to "in humility count others more significant than yourselves" (Philippians 2:3). What would the world look like if I offered the best seat to a stranger, the greater honor to a colleague, or the more important position to a friend? Instead of selecting the hoopskirt of superiority at every opportunity, let's be willing to be the least.

In addition to the hoopskirt, the prom dress of pride will not fit properly without the corset of conceit. In order to carry off the stylish, arrogant look, I must maintain a high opinion of myself. To teach His followers about conceit, Jesus told a parable about a Pharisee and a tax collector who had both gone to the temple to pray (Luke 18:9–14). The Pharisee boldly approached God and reminded Him, "I fast twice a week; I give tithes of all that I get" (v. 12). The Pharisee felt he deserved God's attention because of the good things he had done. I may cringe at his blatant self-acclaim, but I have been guilty of the same thing. I may look at the world around me and think I'm doing pretty well in comparison. Satan may prompt me to take credit for my excellent behavior. My sinful nature may whisper, "No wonder God loves me!"

Jesus continued His story with another character. While the Pharisee was spouting off his accomplishments, a tax collector was praying in another corner of the temple. Tax collectors were even less popular in Jesus' time than they are today, but in this story, he was the one who got God's nod of approval. Was it because of his good deeds and exemplary behavior? No, he received forgiveness and acceptance because he humbly asked God for mercy. He called himself a sinner (v. 13). He realized that on his own, he was sinful and could not hold his head up in God's presence.

In his book *Humility*, Andrew Murray, a pastor in South Africa at the turn of the twentieth century, defined humility as "the sense of entire nothingness, which comes when we see how truly God is all, and in which we make way for God to be all" (Murray, p. 12). When I, like the tax collector, realize I am just a sinner with nothing to offer God and that I am completely unworthy of His love, then I am learning humility. I am ready to wear the willingness to be nothing.

The willingness to be the least and the willingness to be nothing are the foundation garments for our clothing of humility. At first, these undergarments may seem uncomfortable. After all, our natural self—the person we are without Christ—will argue that is much more natural to stand tall in the clothes of superiority and conceit. However, Jesus encourages us to clear our closets of these garments to make room for humility. In the end, humility is the dress that will really make us shine, because we know how imperfect we really are. We know that at the foot of the cross "everyone who exalts himself will be humbled, but the one who humbles himself will be exalted" (Luke 18:14). God Himself will honor those who wear humility.

> *Dear Lord, I admit I want to look better than others. I confess my*
> *tendency to consider myself a better person in comparison to those*
> *around me. Help me to be willing to be less, even to be nothing*
> *in the world's eyes. Then I will be more in Your eyes, which is all*
> *that truly matters. Amen.*

Day Three

Wardrobe Workout

1. Discuss some practical ways to live out the attitudes of willingness to be the least and willingness to be nothing.

2. Christ perfectly modeled humility for us. Read Philippians 2:1–11.

   a. How can we exhibit humility, according to verses 1–5?

   b. Verse 5 states that we should match Jesus' attitude. Look at verses 6–8 and write down some phrases that demonstrate His mind-set.

   c. Study the phrases you just recorded. Prayerfully consider which action God wants you to add to your life this week. Write a short prayer asking the Holy Spirit to work this change in your life.

   d. How does Jesus' life show that God honors those who wear humility (vv. 9–11)?

3. What key lesson did you learn today?

4. Write out this week's memory verse. Try not to peek.

Day Four

◇◇◇◇◇◇◇◇◇◇◇◇◇◇◇◇◇◇◇◇◇

Pitfalls of Pride

But if you will not listen,
My soul will weep in secret for your pride.
Jeremiah 13:17

Our divine Designer advises us that the prom dress of pride is unattractive. The Holy Spirit warns that arrogance is unappealing. If we persist in wearing that gown of pride, we will also experience its pitfalls. Pride will break our connection to God and affect our relationships with other people. Pride is ready to strike anyone, especially those least likely to suspect its trap.

Alienation from God is the first pitfall of pride. Psalm 10:4 (NIV) tells us, "In his pride the wicked does not seek Him; in all his thoughts there is no room for God." Pride separates us from God because it leaves Him out of the picture. The attention-getting ruffles, the hoopskirt of superiority, and the corset of conceit do not let God get close.

Andrew Murray wrote, "Christians may clearly see the blessed promises of perfect peace and rest, of overflowing love and joy, of abiding communion and fruitfulness, yet feel that there is something in-between hindering the true possession. And what might that be? Nothing but pride" (Murray, p. 67). Simply put, pride and faith are incompatible. Faith is having total trust in God after we realize that we can do nothing on our own. Pride will not let us admit that. But when we recognize that God's grace is a gift we do not deserve, we become willing to shed our layers of arrogance and superiority so we can bow down at the cross of Christ and receive His mercy. When we lose the prom dress of pride, we can truly celebrate the compassion of God, rejoice in our Savior's love, and enjoy the close relationship that He wants us to have with Him.

The second pitfall is that pride can distance us from people. In 2 Timothy, Paul records a long list of godless personality traits, including "lovers of self, lovers of money, proud, arrogant, abusive, disobedient to their parents, ungrateful, unholy" (2 Timothy 3:2). Here the Greek word for *proud* is *huperēphanos*, meaning "showing oneself above others" (Vine, p. 292). That hoopskirt of superiority holds others at bay. Think about it: how many people that you would characterize as "full of themselves" do you really want to get close to?

There was a time when I thought I needed to be perfect for people to like me. I imagined that keeping a spotless home and having perfectly behaved children in hand-sewn matching outfits were the keys to attracting friends. In order to appear flawless, I had to try to play down my faults and cover up my mistakes.

Then I met Nina. I was instantly drawn to her and wanted to get to know her better. Did I desire friendship with her because she was perfect? No, my friend Nina laughed about her mistakes and was honest about her shortcomings. I realized that she was a woman I could relate to! I felt comfortable with her. I could be myself. I decided to let everyone in on the fact that I was imperfect (as if they didn't know that already), embrace my flaws and my forgiveness in Christ, and experience freedom from trying to maintain a falsely faultless image. This new attitude liberated me to a new openness and intimacy in my relationships with the wonderful people around me.

The third pitfall of pride is that it is an equal-opportunity weakness. Everyone is susceptible to this disease. In fact, so-called good people may be even more vulnerable to this sin because, well, they're good! They have reason to be pleased with themselves. Satan and our sinful nature will tempt us all to think pridefully about the dignity we have in Christ and the self-esteem we enjoy because of His forgiveness. We become smug about our good character or feel that we are so successful that we are impervious to failure. But Paul warns us that we are just as capable of messing up as anyone: "So, if you think you are standing firm, be careful that you don't fall! No temptation has seized you except what is common to man" (1 Corinthians 10:12–13 NIV). Just when we think we're immune, pride is likely to strike. When we are at the height of our success, we may be tempted to think we can do it on our own. Pride is wearing a tiara with our prom dress when we should cast down our crowns before our King (Revelation 4:10), acknowledging His majesty and our unworthiness.

God tells us that His "soul will weep in secret for your pride" (Jeremiah 13:17). He knows the dangers of arrogance. He is saddened when our pride prevents us from total trust in His goodness and love. He weeps when our bonds with other people are affected by our desire to appear better than them. He knows that the confidence we enjoy in His forgiveness and grace can easily turn into pride in our own good character.

So beware the pitfalls of pride. Examine your heart for any barriers of arrogance. Is there room for God? Is there grace for others? Allow God to knock down any walls of conceit and draw you close to Him.

> *Father, I realize that pride saddens You because it shuts You out of my heart. Help me to be aware when pride is breaking my connection with You or the people I love. Remove any trace of arrogance that pushes You away. In Jesus' name. Amen.*

Day Four

Wardrobe Workout

1. When have you experienced the pitfalls of pride? Describe an instance when pride affected your relationship with God or people in your life.

2. Read Proverbs 29:23. In what ways does contemporary culture conflict with this proverb?

3. What key lesson did you learn today?

4. Write out the memory verse for this week. No peeking!

◇◇◇◇◇◇◇◇◇◇◇◇◇◇◇
Study Styles

A fascinating way to explore the Bible is to do a word study. For instance, to start a word study, look up *pride* or *humility* in a concordance or study Bible and read the verses listed there. You could also use a digital or online Bible such as BibleGateway.com, which has keyword searches and topical indexes, or a commentary that explains in depth the verses and original languages. Once you have read what the Bible says about either of these words, outline the lessons you have learned.

If you do not have time to do an exhaustive search on a topic right now, try a mini word study. Look up the following verses that contain the word *humble* and record the principles about humility you discover.

Deuteronomy 8:2 _____

2 Chronicles 7:14 _____

Psalm 25:9 _____

Proverbs 3:34 _____

Daniel 4:37 _____

Ephesians 4:2 _____

James 4:10 _____

Day Five

◇◇

Practical Ways to Wear Humility

Put on then, as God's chosen ones, holy and beloved, compassionate
hearts, kindness, humility, meekness, and patience.
Colossians 3:12

It has been said, "Humility is like underwear: essential, but indecent if it shows." Once we think we're successful in sporting the clothing of humility, we've actually donned the prom dress of pride again! So what are some sincere ways to wear this essential garment?

The word for *humility* in the New Testament is from the Greek word *tapeinophrosunē*, which means having humility or being modest. Do we accomplish this by putting ourselves down? No. Humility is best accomplished by raising others up.

The first key to true humility is to praise God and elevate Him above our self-interests. David understood that praising the Lord was a means to humility. He wrote, "My soul makes its boast in the LORD; let the humble hear and be glad. Oh, magnify the LORD with me, and let us exalt His name together!" (Psalm 34:2–3). David boasted in the Lord, not in himself. He praised the Lord by magnifying Him. To magnify something is to make it larger. David's song enlarged God in his own eyes and the eyes of others. When God is made greater, we are made smaller in comparison. Praising God is a practical way to wear humility.

When I fix my eyes on my Lord, I am especially aware of His grace. I am astounded by His tenderness and love for me. The suffering He endured in my place moves me to my knees. Then His Holy Spirit may bring to mind things in my heart that need cleaning out. As I confess my sins, I am reminded again of God's free forgiveness and abundant grace. Making confession and receiving God's pardon are practical ways to wear humility.

In addition to elevating God, I can look for opportunities to lift up other people. I can seek out ways to honor others instead of seeking attention for myself. Once, when my children were small, we decided to have a "Dad Is Great" dinner in his honor on an ordinary Friday. We created a banner to hang in the dining room doorway, cooked one of his favorite meals, and made special cards for him. It wasn't a huge effort, but we tried to honor the head of our household in a special way. My friend Linda is exceptionally good at making others feel special. Because of her sincere compliments, I always feel encouraged and blessed after a meeting with Linda. When we show regard for others, we are shedding that hoopskirt of superiority. Honoring others is a practical way to wear humility.

Jesus demonstrated humility for us through servanthood. On the night before His death, Jesus purposefully performed the job of the lowliest slave: He washed His disciples' feet. Did He do this because He thought the disciples' feet were especially dirty? Did He roll up His sleeves and grab the basin of water because He *liked* washing feet? No. Jesus told the disciples, "Now that I, your Lord and Teacher, have washed your feet, you also should wash one another's feet. I have set you an example that you should do as I have done for you" (John 13:14–15 NIV). Jesus took on Himself the lowest and dirtiest job to demonstrate that we should not expect people to wait on us; instead, we should look for opportunities to serve others. This kind of service may not earn financial rewards or enthusiastic applause, but it will please Jesus. This scene also reminds us that only Jesus can wash away the filth of our sins; without His washing and renewal, we walk in sin eternally. Because of Jesus, we serve others with joy, willingness, and humility, because it is one way we can show how Jesus serves us with His perfect love and mercy.

For several years, our church had an after-school program for children. A retired couple from our congregation volunteered to help one day a week. Being with a bunch of squirrelly grade-schoolers who had just been released from sitting in desks all day may not be on everyone's list of top ten enjoyable activities, but these people did it because they wanted to serve. When we bought them a restaurant gift card for Christmas to thank them for their efforts, they chastised us because they felt they were simply following Christ's example of service. Their idea of true servanthood was to give without getting anything in return. Serving without reward is a practical way to wear humility.

We all have events in our lives that take us down a peg or two. Next time this happens, don't despair; instead, look at the experience as a way to grow in humility. A few months ago, someone I knew received a speeding ticket. I was feeling rather smug about my own perfect driving record. Wouldn't you know it, just a month later, I got a ticket. I was driving along a stretch of road known to be a speed trap. I slowed down for the school zone and, when I thought I was out of the restricted zone, I sped up. However, I was driving my husband's car, which has a lot more pickup than my minivan, and before I knew it, I was over the speed limit. (That's my excuse, and I'm sticking to it!) I immediately took my foot off the gas pedal, but it was not soon enough. A police car appeared with the lights flashing. I pulled over, and I soon possessed my first speeding ticket. This was definitely an opportunity to embrace humility. (Oh, by the way, at the first red stoplight I hit afterward, a bird deposited a large blob on my windshield directly in front of my face! Exactly what I was thinking!) Embracing humbling experiences is a practical way to wear humility.

It's time to purge the prom dress of pride from our wardrobes. The hoopskirt of superiority and the corset of conceit are preventing us from growing closer to God. The tiers of self-importance are getting in the way of authentic relationships with other people.

Instead, wear humility by praising God's greatness, confessing your shortcomings, and receiving His grace. Search out ways to honor others and serve without reward. Embrace any humbling opportunities that come your way.

When we are wearing the simple clothing of humility, we are ready to celebrate God's love.

Dear Savior, thank You for Your example of humility. Help me to purge pride from my life. I magnify You and thank You for Your love and mercy. Help me to honor others above myself and serve without seeking anything in return. Amen.

Day Five
Wardrobe Workout

1. Read Ephesians 6:5–8. This passage contains instructions to slaves concerning their life of servitude, but it can also apply to our lives as we learn to serve without reward.

   a. List three attitudes toward service that you find in this passage.

b. What does Paul tell us about the reward for our service?

2. What key lesson did you learn today?

3. Write out 1 Peter 5:5 from memory.

◇◇◇◇◇◇◇◇◇◇◇◇◇◇◇◇◇◇◇◇◇◇◇◇

Meaningful Makeover

We have already seen that "Humility is like underwear, essential, but indecent if it shows." If I ask you if you are humble and you say yes, are you being prideful instead? To check your humility barometer, read the following statements. Do you agree with a statement? Place a plus in front of it. Disagree? Place a minus.

_____ Praising God's greatness and majesty is a regular part of my prayer time.

_____ In my quiet time, I often include confession of my sins and expression of gratitude for God's grace.

_____ I have recently made an effort to honor someone close to me.

_____ When I have accomplished a task, I don't care who gets the credit.

_____ I am willing to serve behind the scenes.

_____ I can laugh at humiliating experiences and accept them as lessons in humility.

How did you do? Is there room for improvement? Choose one of the above aspects of humility that you would like to wear more often. Formulate a plan to put that into action this week.

For example, I want to incorporate praising God into my prayer time. My plan of action: "In my quiet time this week, I will daily pray a psalm of praise to my awesome and amazing Father in heaven."

Aspect of humility: _____

_____

_____

_____

_____

Plan of action: _____

_____

_____

_____

_____

WEEK FIVE

ENVY—Color Consultants Advise: Green Is Out!

Memory Verse

> I know what it is to be in need, and I know what it is to have plenty. I have learned the secret of being content in any and every situation, whether well fed or hungry, whether living in plenty or in want. I can do everything through Him who gives me strength.
>
> Philippians 4:12–13 NIV

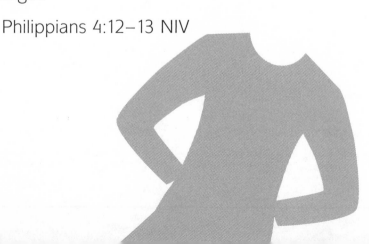

Day One
◇◇◇◇◇◇◇◇◇◇◇◇◇
Envy Green

A tranquil heart gives life to the flesh,
but envy makes the bones rot.
Proverbs 14:30

Have you ever had your colors done? Many years ago, I visited a color consultant who convinced me that I was wearing all the wrong colors. My closet was filled with navy slacks and blue blouses, when my wardrobe should have consisted of warm hues such as brown and red.

Another color the consultant recommended for my coloring was green. Now, my closet holds many shades of green: teal, sage, and forest. There is one shade of green, however, that I work to weed out of my life: envy.

Green is an attractive fashion choice, but our heavenly Color Consultant warns us that we should never be green with envy. That shade of green is not flattering to anyone. So why keep wearing it?

When we moved to Aurora, Illinois, we bought an older home in this Chicago suburb. I had always thought it would be pleasant to live in a quaint old home. Our house, however, did not fit that category. It had all of the problems of a fifty-year-old building but none of the charm.

Although I tried not to complain, this not-so-quaint home left some things to be desired. Large, airy windows gave us a view to our street; however, most of them were painted shut. Upstairs, the bathroom had all the necessary fixtures—toilet, sink, and shower—but only two square feet of floor space. The kitchen came with a functioning stove, but in 1970s harvest gold!

Particularly annoying was the damp, dark basement. The story was that the man who built the house had hand-dug the basement, so it was far from level or even. It varied in height from five feet six inches to six feet, especially irritating to my six-feet-two husband. This basement also leaked. Every time it rained, a puddle the size of Lake Michigan formed at the bottom of the stairs. To get to the washer and dryer, I had to ford this body of water with my laundry basket.

Speaking of laundry, the most bothersome aspect of the house was the water source: a well. At first I thought, Well water—no problem. I had grown up with well water, and we never had any trouble. So my husband hooked up the washer and dryer. I was eager to get some laundry done, because we had been traveling from Montana for several days to get to our new home. I popped in a load of whites, but when they came out of the washer, they were orange! Apparently, there was a lot of iron in the water. This even affected my hair. I usually wash my hair in the shower, and after a short time of sudsing up in this water, I had an orange streak going down the back of my blond hair!

So here I was, living in this old home with its idiosyncrasies, when a new subdivision started up about a mile away. The homes they were building there were all luxury homes—big, beautiful, and brick. I was sure that even the bathrooms in those houses were bigger than my living room. I may not have admitted to out-and-out envy, but driving past those mansions only to park in my crumbling driveway left me dissatisfied. The differences between my home and those homes were all too evident, and soon I had a little green streak in me (to go with the orange one in my hair).

Looking back on my life, I see that envy-green was a color I often wore. In first grade, I was envious when the teacher gave Susie the part of the bride-doll in the school play. She got to wear a bridal costume, while I was stuck with the part of the narrator and didn't get to wear *any* costume, just my usual clothes. In junior high, I was jealous of the girls who were the first to graduate out of their training bras. In high school, the popular girls got all the attention from students and faculty and were elected homecoming queen or "most popular"—and I wore green again.

I thought envy was my only choice in those situations. After all, other people had something I wanted. Jealousy of their good fortune was natural. Desire for the same benefits and blessings was to be expected. Resentment was normal, right?

But envy "makes the bones rot" (Proverbs 14:30), and over time I realized that discontent had devoured my happiness. It swallowed up my excitement for life. It consumed my joy and left me with only the heartburn of frustration.

I had yet to learn that contentment "gives life to the body" (Proverbs 14:30 NIV). Satisfaction in less than perfect circumstances seemed impossible. I didn't realize that God teaches me to be content, whatever the state of my affairs or circumstances.

God is the expert teacher, of course. In His Holy Word, our divine Designer instructs us how to eliminate envy through avoiding comparison with other people and counting our own blessings: "Turn away from evil and do good; seek peace and pursue it" (Psalm 34:14). The apostle Paul reminds us that "love is patient and kind;

love does not envy or boast; it is not arrogant or rude" (1 Corinthians 13:4–5). Who among us would rather feel envy than love?

Our Creator will help us discover that He is more than enough. The Holy Spirit gives us faith to believe that "the peace of God, which passes all understanding" (Philippians 4:7), is ours through Christ. He is more than all we desire. He will help us toss out all the envy-green garments in our closets to make room for the color of contentment.

> *Giver of all good gifts, in this world it is so easy for me to focus on what I don't have. Help me to overcome envy in my life. Enable me to develop an attitude of contentment. I pray in Jesus' name. Amen.*

Day One
Wardrobe Workout

1. Search your wardrobe for an item in a shade of green. Compare your green garment to the others in your group. Which item do you like best? Do you agree that comparing yourself or your circumstances can lead to envy and dissatisfaction? Why or why not?

2. Read James 3:13–18. This passage contrasts God's wisdom with envy.

   a. How do we often display envy (v. 14)?

b. How does this passage characterize envy (v. 15)?

c. What are some results of envy (v. 16)?

d. God's wisdom is the antidote to envy and selfish ambition. What are some characteristics of this wisdom (vv. 13, 17)?

3. What key lesson did you learn today?

4. Our memory verse for this week is Philippians 4:12–13 (NIV): "I know what it is to be in need, and I know what it is to have plenty. I have learned the secret of being content in any and every situation, whether well fed or hungry, whether living in plenty or in want. I can do everything through Him who gives me strength." To help you memorize this passage, write it out in the space below.

Day Two

◇◇◇◇◇◇◇◇◇◇◇◇◇◇◇◇◇◇◇◇◇◇◇◇◇◇◇◇◇◇◇◇◇◇◇◇

What's So Bad about Envy?

Resentment kills a fool, and envy slays the simple.
Job 5:2 NIV

Envy is a natural emotion, correct? So what's so bad about it? What's wrong with looking at what someone else has and wishing a little of it might come our way? After all, we're only human.

In his Letter to the Romans, the apostle Paul wrote about some serious offenders. He described them as being "filled with all manner of unrighteousness, evil, covetousness, malice" (1:29a). That sounds pretty scandalous. Exactly what were they doing? Paul goes on to tell us, "They are full of envy, murder, strife, deceit, maliciousness" (1:29b). Whoa! The *first* offense listed is envy—even before murder! I think we can agree that envy is not just a misdemeanor in God's book.

What is envy, specifically? The Greek word for envy here in Romans is *phthonos*, which is translated into English as jealousy or envy and is used in a negative sense. Envy is feeling a pinch of pain when someone else is experiencing something we desire. It can even be as extreme as a desire for evil on those who are enjoying the pleasures we crave. In this materialistic age, envy often appears in the form of dissatisfaction with our financial status. We can also battle discontent with our physical appearance, personality, friends, family relationships, or career. In any form, envy is an attitude that does not please God.

Do you remember the Ninth Commandment? "You shall not covet your neighbor's house" (Exodus 20:17). This is what Luther said about the Ninth Commandment in his Small Catechism: "We should fear and love God so that we do not scheme to get our neighbor's inheritance or house, or get it in a way which only appears right, but help and be of service to him in keeping it." The commentary on this commandment defines *coveting* as "sinful desire" and tells us where it comes from: "sin . . . produced in me every kind of covetous desire" (Romans 7:8 NIV; see *Luther's Small Catechism with Explanation*, Question 63).

Envy can lead to even more serious problems with the people in our lives. James, the brother of Jesus, talked about the effects of envy on our relationships. He wrote:

> What causes fights and quarrels among you? Don't they come from
> your desires that battle within you? You want something but don't
> get it. You kill and covet, but you cannot have what you want. You
> quarrel and fight. (James 4:1–2 NIV)

Jealousy, envy, and coveting can certainly lead to squabbles and disagreements. How many friendships have suffered from the effects of envy?

In an article for MentalHealth.net, psychologist Nancy Staats Reiss, PhD, writes about the mental, physical, and emotional results of envy, saying that it can be detrimental to a person's overall health and destructive to one's relationships (Reiss, "The Nature of Envy," MentalHealth.Net). Our good feelings toward others will sour if we let envy take over. We cannot feel happiness for the person who has what we desperately want. Our attitude will show. Back in first grade, I certainly was not thinking warm, loving thoughts toward Susie when she strutted across the stage in her bridal costume, while I was stuck behind the podium in my everyday clothes!

When I first pull on my favorite envy-green outfit, I simply desire what another person has. But if I continue to wear that outfit, my feelings can develop into contempt for the other person because he or she is a reminder of what I don't have. If I refuse to take off my green suit, the feeling can lead to malice: wanting to destroy the good in the other person's life. After all, if I can't experience the pleasure I want, the other person shouldn't be able to, either. Envy can destroy our relationships with other people.

Kermit the Frog sang about the difficulties of "being green." Don't you agree? Envy not only displeases God and damages human relationships, but it can also demolish our own happiness. The attitude of dissatisfaction will ultimately cause emotional pain. In her article on "The Nature of Envy," Dr. Reiss also wrote that just as envy leads to resentment and anger, it is also related to depression, anxiety, and personal unhappiness.

We find this same teaching in the Bible. Job 5:2 (NIV) states, "Resentment kills a fool, and envy slays the simple." Resenting what others have will kill my enjoyment of life. Envy will destroy any chance of happiness. Concentrating on what I think is missing in my life will lead only to misery and stress. How many nights have I lost sleep over something I thought I desperately needed in my life?

Resentment and envy will slaughter my joy and pleasure. When I focused on the popular girls in high school, my happiness fizzled. Focusing on the good friends that God has provided in every stage of my life could have brought joy and satisfaction. Envy can rob us of our joy and lead to quarreling, which destroys relationships with people we love. Discontent and resentment can lead to depression and anger, erasing our happiness.

Envy displeases God. When I focus on what I do not have, I display discontent with what my heavenly Father has wisely and lovingly provided. My envy shows that although God has given me much, I don't think it is enough.

It gets worse. James 1:14–15 tells us that "each one is tempted when, by his own evil desire, he is dragged away and enticed. Then, after desire has conceived, it gives birth to sin; and sin, when it is full-grown, gives birth to death." Envy can jeopardize my relationship with my Savior.

It's time to recognize envy for what it is: a killer. It slays relationships and executes joy. How do we omit envy and find a life of joy? By focusing on the gifts God has already provided and allowing an attitude of contentment to bloom within us. Our creative God has provided us with so much beauty and joy, which are ours without measure and without cost to us. As the psalmist said, "Delight yourself in the LORD, and He will give you the desires of your heart" (Psalm 37:4).

When we understand that God's mercies are new every morning and that He will always bless us beyond our imagination, then we know what contentment is. What else could we possibly want?

> *Heavenly Father, I am sorry for the times when my discontent has shown a disappointment in what You have given me. Free me from this attitude, which harms my relationships with You and the people in my life. Release me from envy and give me joy. In Jesus' name. Amen.*

Day Two
◇◇◇◇◇◇◇◇◇◇◇◇◇◇◇◇◇◇◇◇◇◇
Wardrobe Workout

1. What does the statement "Envy can rob us of our joy" mean in the context of your life?

2. Asaph, one of the temple choir directors during the time of King David, wrote an open and honest admission of his own envy in Psalm 73. Read his confession and answer the following questions.

   a. What caused Asaph's envy (v. 3)?

   b. What was Asaph's view of those he envied (vv. 4–12)? How do you perceive the people you envy?

   c. How did envy cause Asaph to stumble (vv. 2, 13–16, 21–22)? Do you think that envy can change your relationships with God and with other people? Can you think of a time when that has happened in your life? Write about it here.

d. What changed Asaph's attitude (vv. 17–20)? When you struggle with envy or jealousy, what do you do to alter your outlook?

e. Contrast Asaph's desires in the beginning of the psalm (v. 3) with his longings at the end (vv. 23–28). What principle of contentment can you glean from these verses?

3. What key lesson did you learn today?

4. Write out our memory verse for this week: "I know what it is to be in need, and I know what it is to have plenty. I have learned the secret of being content in any and every situation, whether well fed or hungry, whether living in plenty or in want. I can do everything through Him who gives me strength" (Philippians 4:12–13 NIV). Write it out phrase by phrase, trying to do as much of it as you can from memory.

Day Three

⬢⬢⬢⬢⬢⬢⬢⬢⬢⬢⬢⬢

A Tale of Two Sisters

*Be still before the L*ORD *and wait patiently for Him;*
fret not yourself over the one who prospers in his way.
Psalm 37:7

Once upon a time, there were two sisters living in the home of their father.
The older sister had weak eyes; the younger one was beautiful. One day, a long-
lost cousin came to visit and fell in love at first sight with one of these two young
women. (Guess which one!) Their father took his nephew into the family business
and eventually asked what wage the young man would like to be paid. The nephew
worked up his courage and asked that his pay be the hand of the younger daughter
in marriage. (Did you guess right?) The father agreed, and things went along just
fine until the wedding night. When the time came to consummate the marriage, the
father pulled a switcheroo and substituted the older sister, placing her in the wedding tent. The young man must have overindulged in the wedding punch, because
he didn't notice the substitution until the next morning! He angrily confronted his
uncle, who tried to patch up the situation by offering his younger daughter as wife
number two! As you might guess, this story did not end with "and they lived happily
ever after."

Perhaps you recognize this tale as the Old Testament story of Jacob, who traveled to visit his uncle Laban and worked for seven years as payment for the privilege
of marrying Rachel, was tricked into marrying Leah, the older sister, instead, and
then worked another seven years after he was granted permission to marry Rachel.
Of course, this situation was doomed. Matters grew worse "when the LORD saw that
Leah was hated, He opened her womb, but Rachel was barren" (Genesis 29:31).
Each woman was envious of what the other had. Leah wanted her husband's love
more than anything else, and Rachel was desperate for children. Both sisters donned
their most garish green envy outfits and made their lives miserable.

The names chosen for the children born during this time reflect the misery the
women felt. Leah named her first son *Reuben*, which sounds like the Hebrew for "He
has seen my misery." She said, "Because the LORD has looked upon my affliction; for
now my husband will love me" (v. 32). When her second son was born, Leah said,

"Because the LORD has heard that I am hated, He has given me this son also" (v. 33); she named him *Simeon*, which means "one who hears." Leah named her third son *Levi*, which sounds like a Hebrew term that means "attached," and Leah said, "Now this time my husband will be attached to me, because I have borne him three sons" (v. 34). Reading the account in Genesis, I get the impression that Leah felt little joy in the birth of her sons, only envy and misery, because of the lack of her husband's love.

In the meantime, Rachel was waiting, not so patiently, for her first child. At one point, she became so jealous of her sister that she pleaded with Jacob, "Give me children, or I shall die!" (Genesis 30:1). Jacob probably said something like, "Look, I'm doing all I can, but I'm not God!" So Rachel decided to take matters into her own hands (never a good idea). She gave Jacob her maid, Bilhah, as his concubine. Then Bilhah became pregnant with Jacob's son and presented him to Rachel. This precious baby was called *Dan*, meaning "he vindicated," because Rachel said, "God has vindicated me" (v. 6). Funny how when things turn out the way we want, we think that God must approve! Bilhah's second pregnancy resulted in another son, whom Rachel named *Naphtali*, meaning "my struggle," for she declared, "I have wrestled with my sister and have prevailed" (v. 8). Rachel was letting envy destroy her relationship with her sister.

Talk about a dysfunctional family. But Leah and Rachel were not the only ones to blame. Laban was the one who got them into the whole mess, and from the looks of it, Jacob was not helping to smooth things out. These sisters exacerbated the situation; each one concentrated on what she didn't have. This story would not rate a "happily ever after" ending, but these men and women could have experienced more joy and satisfaction if the sisters had learned the secret of eliminating envy.

Psalm 37:7 cautions us against getting upset when someone else "prospers in his way." It's so easy to lose sight of what we have when we look only at what our sister has. Leah had children; Rachel had Jacob's love. Neither was happy because each lacked what the other possessed.

Instead, the psalmist tells us, "Be still before the LORD and wait patiently for Him." Rather than longing for what our sister has that we don't, let's wait for God's plan for us to unfold. Although it is difficult to be patient, the account of Leah and Rachel clearly demonstrates that envy does not improve a situation. Our heavenly Father knows our hearts' desires. He will provide for our needs and even our wants, but He asks that we trust Him. While we wait for His timing, let's be thankful for the blessings He has already given us and let's receive Him through His Means of Grace.

Lord Jesus, help me to keep my eyes on You instead of on what others have that I don't. I want to trust in You. Give me patience to wait for Your timing. Amen.

Day Three

◇◇◇◇◇◇◇◇◇◇◇◇◇◇◇◇◇◇◇◇

Wardrobe Workout

1. Using the "Content-o-meter" below, fill in the graph from the bottom up to where your level of contentment is presently.

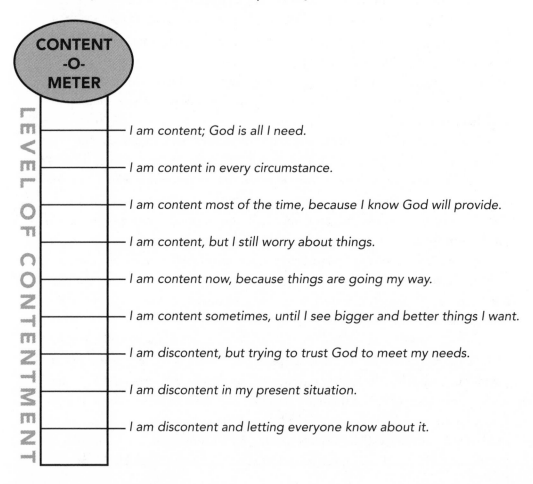

CONTENT -O- METER

LEVEL OF CONTENTMENT

— *I am content; God is all I need.*

— *I am content in every circumstance.*

— *I am content most of the time, because I know God will provide.*

— *I am content, but I still worry about things.*

— *I am content now, because things are going my way.*

— *I am content sometimes, until I see bigger and better things I want.*

— *I am discontent, but trying to trust God to meet my needs.*

— *I am discontent in my present situation.*

— *I am discontent and letting everyone know about it.*

What determined your current contentment level? Was it circumstances? comparisons? feelings? connection to God?

Write a prayer asking the Holy Spirit to help you reach the next level of contentment.

What practical steps can you take to increase your satisfaction? (Some ideas might be canceling your subscription to *Better Homes and Gardens* or staying away from the mall for a week.)

2. Today we read part 1 of the Leah and Rachel story, found in Genesis 29:1–30:8. Now read part 2 of their saga in Genesis 30:9–24. Pay attention to the meanings of the names of their children, given in the notes in your study Bible.

   a. Observing the names of the children, what do you learn about the thinking of Rachel and Leah? Have they changed their attitudes?

   b. In the Old Testament, multiple wives and concubines were common, but the practice was not endorsed by God. If you were an Old Testament marriage counselor trying to make the best out of a bad situation, what advice might you offer these two women?

3. What key lesson did you learn today?

4. Write out this week's memory verse. Try not to peek.

Day Four

The Color of Contentment

*I know what it is to be in need, and I know what it is
to have plenty. I have learned the secret of being content in any
and every situation, whether well fed or hungry,
whether living in plenty or in want.*
Philippians 4:12 NIV

Savvy color consultants are able to analyze your features and skin tone and recommend colors and hues that will enhance your attractiveness—or make you look like a sick fish! Our divine Color Consultant, the Holy Spirit, advises us that we are at our loveliest when we eliminate envy-green from our wardrobes and wear the color of contentment instead.

One day, when I was still struggling with envy in my house-that-turned-hair-orange, I read what the apostle Paul wrote to the Philippians, "I have learned in whatever situation I am to be content" (4:11). Immediately, I knew that God was telling me what was missing from my life.

Did contentment come naturally to Paul? I don't think so. After all, Paul wrote those words while he was stuck in prison. Prisons being what they were, two thousand years ago, I can't imagine that it was easy finding satisfaction in those circumstances. But he told the Philippians that because of Christ's work in his life, he had learned contentment. The Greek word for *learn* is *manthanō*, which can mean to learn, especially hands-on learning, or to grow in knowledge. Paul may have struggled with thoughts of self-pity and frustration, yet he disciplined himself to replace them continually with reasons to praise and thank God. Through faith, Paul was able to wear contentment more easily than dissatisfaction. I am encouraged by this, because if Paul could learn contentment, perhaps I can too.

The Greek word Paul used for *content* is *autarkēs*, meaning "self-sufficient." Paul had learned to be satisfied with whatever situation he was in. He tells the Philippians, "I know what it is to be in need, and I know what it is to have plenty. I have learned the secret of being content in any and every situation, whether well fed or hungry, whether living in plenty or in want" (4:12 NIV). Personally, I'm not sure how he managed contentment on an empty stomach. I get pretty grouchy when my stomach is growling. Yet Paul—and remember, he was in prison when he wrote this Letter to the Philippians—said he had learned the secret to being content in *any* situation.

What was that secret? Paul didn't keep it to himself. He shares it with us: "I can do all things through Him who strengthens me" (v. 13 NIV). The secret is not self-sufficiency but sufficiency in Christ. Paul knew he was not able to wear contentment consistently on his own; only Jesus could give him the power to live each day in satisfaction. His Savior offered the strength to see beyond current circumstances and recognize God was with him, then and in eternity. Christ gave him the ability to put on the color of contentment instead of envy-green each day and in every circumstance.

Look again at that Greek word for *content*. The root word for *autarkēs* is *arkeō*, which describes the attitude of being satisfied with what is available. Paul looked at what he did have in Christ. God was always available to him, and he learned to be content with that. Paul knew that "God will supply every need of yours according to His riches in glory in Christ Jesus" (Philippians 4:19).

This is the key to learning contentment. We, like Paul, need to recognize that God really is enough. As a child, I loved hearing Psalm 23 read and recited. I could picture a gentle Shepherd leading His woolly lambs to a bubbling brook surrounded by gently rolling hills covered with lush green grass. I imagined the lambs playfully nipping at the Shepherd's heels and resting at His side. But the first phrase always puzzled me: "The LORD is my shepherd; I shall not want" (KJV). What could that mean? Didn't David want God to be his shepherd? Did he want a different shepherd?

Eventually, I asked my mother about that verse. Exactly what did "I shall not want" mean? I remember her telling me that because God was David's shepherd, David didn't want anything else. My small-child brain tried to take that in. Okay, that made more sense than not wanting Jesus for a shepherd, but how could he not want anything else? Didn't he want food or clothes? How could you not want friends and family or hot fudge sundaes or Barbie dolls?

Many of our more modern versions of the Bible phrase Psalm 23:1 this way: "The LORD is my shepherd, I shall not be in want" (NIV). Psalm 23 describes the perfect Shepherd, the consummate Provider. I am not in want, because He anticipates what I require for this life and for the life to come. I have everything I need, because the Lord generously supplies what is necessary for my body today and for my soul tomorrow. I acknowledge this every time I ask God for "daily bread" and receive the refreshment Christ freely gives in His body and blood. I may not get all the hot fudge sundaes I want, but God, in His wisdom, imparts what is best for me. I find contentment when I trust my Good Shepherd to provide what I require and what I long for.

Now I know that my mother was right. True contentment is found when God is all I desire, when I long for His nearness more than for a new house, when I crave Him more than hot fudge sundaes. Of course, even though I am all grown up now, I still struggle with this truth. In this world, due to human nature, desire for large bank accounts and spacious homes seems more attractive than longing for God. Aspirations for success and recognition appear more logical than desiring closeness with an invisible Creator. Even wishing for cute shoes and designer bags sometimes competes with my yearning for my Savior. But when I find true satisfaction in my Shepherd and trust Him to provide what I need, I do find contentment. My prayer is that I always wear the color of contentment.

Good Shepherd, thank You for providing for my needs. Forgive
me when I forget that You are more than all I desire. Help me to

learn contentment and live each day in satisfaction. In Your Holy name. Amen.

Day Four

◇◇◇◇◇◇◇◇◇◇◇◇◇◇◇◇◇◇◇◇◇

Wardrobe Workout

1. Let's explore the meaning of *contentment* today.

   a. Write down your first reaction to this question: How do you define *contentment*?

   b. Look up the word *contentment* in a dictionary and write out the definition.

   c. Using your own definition, the dictionary definition, and the meaning of the Greek words *autarkēs* and *arkeō* (see p. 127), come up with a practical description of contentment and write it here.

   d. Describe the contentment you feel as you kneel at the Lord's Table. What does our Lord give you there?

2. What key lesson did you learn today?

3. Write out the memory verse for this week. No peeking!

◇◇◇◇◇◇◇◇◇◇◇◇
Study Styles

Personalizing Scripture can be a meaningful study aid. Psalm 23 is a wonderful creed of contentment, a well-known song of comfort. Meditate on each verse and put it into your own words in light of what you have learned about contentment. Rephrase each verse, beginning each sentence with the words "I am content because _____" or "I can be content because _____." For example, "The LORD is my shepherd; I shall not want" could be stated as, "I am content because God is my Shepherd; God is almighty, all-knowing, and has unlimited resources. He is more than able to meet my needs."

Verse 1: "The LORD is my Shepherd; I shall not want."

Verse 2: "He makes me lie down in green pastures. He leads me beside still waters."

Verse 3: "He restores my soul. He leads me in paths of righteousness for His name's sake."

Verse 4: "Even though I walk through the valley of the shadow of death, I will fear no evil, for You are with me; Your rod and Your staff, they comfort me."

Verse 5: "You prepare a table before me in the presence of my enemies; You anoint my head with oil; my cup overflows."

Verse 6: "Surely goodness and mercy shall follow me all the days of my life, and I shall dwell in the house of the LORD forever."

Day Five
Whose Blessings Are You Counting?

The one who offers thanksgiving as his sacrifice glorifies Me;
to one who orders his way rightly
I will show the salvation of God!
Psalm 50:23

Have you heard it said, "Envy is the art of counting the other fellow's blessings rather instead of your own"? Let's see, my sister has twenty-five pairs of shoes, my friend has three designer handbags, and my co-worker has, well, more sweaters than I can count. Oh, there I go again!

In order to keep my envy-green outfits out of my closet, I need to avoid making comparisons. The sin of envy comes from looking at what others have rather than keeping my eye on my own reasons to be thankful. Consider Galatians 6:4, which reminds us to "let each one test his own work, and then his reason to boast will be in himself alone and not in his neighbor," and 1 Timothy 6:6, "Now there is great gain in godliness with contentment."

Back in first grade, I was initially excited to be given the part of narrator. I became dissatisfied only when I saw Susie's costume and the admiration she received for her beauty. At first, I was pleased that the teacher thought enough of my reading ability to trust me with the narrator part, but when I compared it to the glamour of the bride-doll role, my happiness fizzled.

Even now it is easy for me to feel like a failure when I compare my work to the success of Oprah Winfrey, my bank account to Bill Gates's, or my reputation to the fame of Julia Roberts. Yet when I quit evaluating my life against the success or failure of others, I see that God has given me countless gifts and opportunities.

Instead of counting other women's blessings, I eventually learned to take time to count my own. When I was struggling to find happiness in a house that turned my hair orange, I certainly was not finding it while gazing at the gazillion-dollar homes down the road. But those homes were not available to me: my budget didn't come close! What was available was an older home with a few idiosyncrasies. I learned to look past the windows that didn't open and the leaky basement. I practiced contentment by thanking God for the fact that we had a roof over our heads. I reminded myself of the good points of our home: it was warm and cozy and roomy enough for our family; we had a large yard and lived across the street from a park, where our children loved to play.

It isn't easy to be thankful when things are not going the way I want. A few months ago I discovered this verse: "The one who offers thanksgiving as his sacrifice glorifies Me; to one who orders his way rightly I will show the salvation of God!" (Psalm 50:23). Sometimes it may be a real sacrifice to come up with words of thankfulness, but when I do, I honor my Shepherd by demonstrating to Him that I trust His provision and His timing. I may still feel needy; I may still think I lack something crucial for my happiness. However, as I express gratitude for the gifts I already have and the gifts that I know will be mine in eternity, I am honoring the Giver and preparing my heart to see Him and His continuous saving grace in my life. I pray that God will strengthen my trust in Him to supply what will truly satisfy me. I ask my Shepherd to open my eyes to the blessings in my life and give me victory in the struggle for contentment.

My daughter, Anna, is already a good example of contentment. (She must get it from her dad.) Right now, she and her little family are living halfway around the world, in China. Some of the luxuries not included in their apartment are a kitchen stove, a sink, and a fully functioning bathroom door! She seemed a little discouraged when they first moved in, but she thanked God for the amenities they do have: a Western-style toilet, one heated room, and high-speed Internet—very important to parents left behind! She recognizes how much more they have than many of their neighbors. Her attitude of contentment inspires me as she adapts to a life in a foreign culture.

We can express our love for our Provider and exhibit trust in His timing and supply by showing gratitude for our many blessings. One way to count your blessings is to write prayers of thankfulness in a gratitude notebook. Record big things such as your home and your job, but don't forget small things such as your warm fuzzy robe or a beautiful sunset. My daily prayers of thanks include my faithful and supportive husband, children, and grandchildren. But I also regularly express my appreciation for a luxuriously soft bed and a microwave that can heat my tea in two minutes!

It's so easy to put on the little green outfit when we are envious of all the jeweled and sequined numbers everyone else seems to be wearing! But let's remember: an envy suit truly dishonors God. An attitude of discontent demonstrates distrust in God's provision for our lives. That little green streak shouts loud and clear that we think God has not given us enough. Recall that envy is a destructive emotion, damaging our relationships with other people and demolishing our own joy.

Instead, let's continue on the journey of "God is enough," learning that the secret of contentment that Paul wrote to us about is in Christ's perfect provision. Avoid comparing your life, your home, your husband, or your kids to those of the women around you. The attitude of contentment is fueled by thankfulness and gratitude, so remember to count your own blessings. Enjoy what God has already given you—participation in His glory, which we possess through our Baptism—and avoid the constant quest for more. It's easy to wear envy-green, but that color will never be "in," never flatter, and never coordinate with the image of Christ. Wear the color of contentment in Him instead.

Dear Lord, I offer You the sacrifice of thanksgiving. I thank You
for my current situation, good or bad, for I know You love me and

*are working everything for my good. Help me to count my own
blessings and not someone else's. Amen.*

Day Five
Wardrobe Workout

1. Today we read, "The one who offers thanksgiving as his sacrifice glorifies Me"
   (Psalm 50:23).

   a. Give God thanks for the blessings in your life by writing a list of some of the
   things for which you are grateful.

   b. Some blessings require a sacrifice of thanksgiving. Do you have any of
   these blessings in your life right now? If you are ready to make that sacrifice, write a prayer of thanksgiving for them here:

2. Read Colossians 3:2–5, 11.

   a. What does this passage say to you about those who have and those who
   have not?

b. What do the words "Christ is all, and in all" mean to you today?

3. What key lesson did you learn today?

4. Write out Philippians 4:12–13 from memory.

◇◇◇◇◇◇◇◇◇◇◇◇◇◇◇◇◇◇◇◇◇◇◇◇◇◇◇◇◇◇

Meaningful Makeover

Envy and dissatisfaction can attack us in many different areas. The following boxes represent the different departments of our lives. Examine your heart. Are you experiencing discontent in any of these areas? If so, write down any specific items that bring feelings of dissatisfaction. For instance, in the department of finance, you might write, "not enough money for a family vacation," or in the department of friends, you might desire one close friend who shares your Christian faith. Then hunt through this chapter and your Bible for verses that will help you overcome your discontent.

Finances	**Physical Appearance**	**Personality**

Friends	**Family Relationships**	**Career**

Remember to bring your green outfit to your group's meeting!

WEEK SIX

SELFISHNESS—Boot Out the Boots

Memory Verse

This is how we know what love is: Jesus Christ laid down His life for us. And we ought to lay down our lives for our brothers.

1 John 3:16 NIV

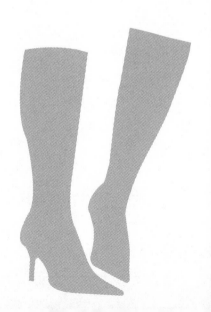

Day One

◇◇◇

These Boots Are Made for Walkin'

Let no one seek his own good, but the good of his neighbor.
1 Corinthians 10:24

In the hazy spotlight of the corner streetlamp, three preteen girls moved to the music that rang out from the nearby portable record player. Hair flying, arms waving, and hips swaying, their feet stomped on the concrete driveway to the beat of "These Boots Are Made for Walkin'."

Summer was our season. Mary, Jeanie, and I didn't see much of each other during the school year because we all went to different schools, but come June, we splashed in the neighborhood creek, set up a lemonade stand, or played with our Barbie dolls in the basement rec room.

One year, we had the great idea to put on a variety show for our parents. We spent a couple of weeks brainstorming ideas for the show, hunting for jokes in old *Reader's Digest* magazines, and rehearsing our skits and dance numbers. Our skits were very cerebral. In one scene, I acted as a patron of a restaurant. Jeanie took my order for soup and swiftly set a bowl in front of me on the card table prop. I began to eat, but suddenly I stopped and screamed, "Waiter, there's a fly in my soup!" and immediately, I yanked a big plastic fly out of the water in the bowl. At every rehearsal, we snorted with laughter. (Go figure.)

We also wanted to be sure to include the old pie-in-the-face gag, but we didn't know what we could use for the pie without arousing our parents' suspicion. Ultimately we decided that one of the girls would sneak her father's shaving cream out of the bathroom and squirt it into an aluminum pie plate. Poor Mary was the recipient of the eye-stinging mess!

Finally, the big night arrived. The stage? Our driveway. Seating? Lawn chairs. Refreshments? Popcorn and lemonade. Our big dance number was the finale. Jeanie had the popular new record by Nancy Sinatra. Our arms flailed in an effort to dance the Monkey. Our heads bobbed and swayed. Our feet did their very best to imitate the moves we saw on *American Bandstand*. All the while, Nancy's voice rang out from the record player, "These Boots Are Made for Walkin'."

We had a blast and our parents enjoyed the evening of home-grown entertainment. It was a great way to spend our summer vacation.

Lately, I've been thinking that Nancy Sinatra's old song pretty much sums up how we treat one another in this world. Children push and shove to get to the front of the line. In the business world, boots step on toes on the way up the corporate ladder. Shoppers get trampled to death at Wal-Mart in an attempt to obtain Christmas bargains.

Wearing our boots of selfishness and tromping on others to get our own way seems so natural. In fact, it is part of the human condition. Since the moment Adam and Eve listened to the serpent's lies, we humans have been more concerned about ourselves than about those around us. Adam and Eve's son Cain killed his brother Abel in anger. When God confronted Cain, asking, "Where is Abel your brother?" Cain replied, "Am I my brother's keeper?" (Genesis 4:9). Cain did not recognize that yes, he was his brother's keeper.

In the same way, I am also my brother's keeper. The Bible says, "Let no one seek his own good, but the good of his neighbor" (1 Corinthians 10:24). Instead of thinking only about myself, I am to be concerned about others too. Pleasing myself should take a back seat to pleasing others. Helping my neighbor should be a habit, not an occasional event.

Jesus gave us a clear example of this in His parable of the Good Samaritan in Luke 10:30–37, admonishing us to extend care to all people, not just to those we love or who are like us. As we consider this parable in a broader sense, we realize that Jesus is the ultimate Good Samaritan. Jesus is the one who kneels to lift us from the ditch of defeat and who provides the soothing balm of forgiveness for our wounds. He paid the ultimate price for our restoration.

I can't abandon the boots of selfishness alone. But Christ helps me to put on shoes of love instead of selfishness. With Jesus, I am able to wear shoes of sacrifice instead of self-centeredness. These new shoes will be shoes of life, bringing a spring to my step and energy to my days. Walking through life will be much easier with shoes of grace and purpose. Instead of walking all over you, I will walk toward you, ready to serve you in Jesus' name!

> *Heavenly Father, my human nature tends to walk over other*
> *people instead of caring for them. Help me to see the people in my*
> *life as You see them. May I see their needs and not just my own.*
> *In Jesus' name. Amen.*

Day One
◇◇◇◇◇◇◇◇◇◇◇◇◇◇◇◇◇◇◇◇◇◇
Wardrobe Workout

1. Do you own a pair of boots? Bring your snow boots, ankle boots, or go-go boots to your group meeting. Discuss an aspect of your boots and how this feature could be related to selfishness. For instance, if I owned a pair of purple boots, I would mention their attention-getting color. Selfishness demands that all attention be directed toward me. (For fun, you might want to watch Nancy Sinatra sing "These Boots Were Made for Walkin'" on YouTube.)

2. How do you define selfishness?

3. Read Genesis 4:1–12.

   a. Since God knows everything, why do you think He asked Cain, "Where is Abel your brother?" (v. 9).

b. What attitude(s) does Cain reveal by his response, "Am I my brother's keeper?" (v. 9).

c. Do you see yourself as your brother's keeper? How does your attitude toward your brother show itself in your daily life?

d. If we all lived as keepers of our brothers and sisters, how would life be different here on earth?

4. What key lesson did you learn today?

5. Our memory verse for this week is 1 John 3:16 (NIV): "This is how we know what love is: Jesus Christ laid down His life for us. And we ought to lay down our lives for our brothers." To help you memorize this verse, write it out in the space below.

Day Two
◇◇◇◇◇◇◇◇◇◇◇◇◇◇◇◇◇◇
Boots That Pinch

Let each of us please his neighbor for his good, to build him up.
Romans 15:2

Sometimes children tell us more about ourselves than we would like them to or than we are willing to admit.

A friend told me about a scene she witnessed in her church. Just a few pews ahead of her, a young couple was sitting with their three-year-old son. The tyke was well behaved until it came time for the offering. When the ushers came to their pew, they handed the plate to Dad, who sent it on to Mom, who passed it to her son. Junior took hold of the plate, noticed what was in it, and clutched it tight. He did not want to pass it on. In fact, an usher had to sidle down the pew and wrestle it out of his hands!

We're expected to outgrow selfish tendencies. Yet, if I'm honest, when an opportunity to share my gifts with others comes into my life, how often do I look into it and ask myself, "What do I get in exchange?"

Our society encourages this. Commercials urge us to be self-sufficient and self-indulgent. Pop-psychology classes teach self-esteem and self-assurance. No one is surprised if we are self-serving or self-promoting. Popular talk shows feature guests who promise to help us find self-fulfillment and elevate our self-confidence. Bookstore shelves are lined with titles such as *Learning to Love Yourself: Finding Your Self-Worth, Honoring the Self*, and *Ten Days to Self-Esteem*. What do all these have in common?

Self.

Certainly, I am no different. I have bought my fair share of self-help books and watched a few episodes of Dr. Phil in hopes of improving myself and boosting my self-confidence. Lately, though, I've been wondering if my search for self-fulfillment is not fulfilling because the "self" part is the problem and not the solution.

In his book *Blue Like Jazz*, Donald Miller talks about a conversation he had with a friend about racism. Miller expressed the opinion that the problem was greater than just friction between cultures and races. He told his friend, "I'm talking about self-absorption. If you think about it, the human race is pretty self-absorbed. Racism might be the symptom of a greater disease" (Miller, pp. 46–47). In other words, self-absorption or selfishness is the cause of a host of our other problems. We can trace not only racism but also crimes such as robbery and murder to selfish desires. Even global problems such as war and hunger could be avoided if human beings were not so self-absorbed.

I once bought a beautiful pair of brown leather boots. Because I lived in Wisconsin, the boots were a practical purchase, but I also wanted them to look good. Stylish they were, but not very comfortable. I was hesitant about purchasing the chocolate-colored footwear because they felt tight in the toe and loose in the heel. However, the sales person assured me that since they were leather, they would soon be broken in, mold to my feet, and fit like a soft glove. That never happened. Every time I wore those boots, they pinched my toes and rubbed blisters on my heels.

I think selfishness is like that. Although we wear our self-absorption every day, it never becomes truly comfortable. Sure, it may be fashionable and attractive to the world around us, but it never quite satisfies us. Self-help, self-esteem, and self-confidence books keep selling because they fix the problem temporarily, but they don't fulfill our true need. Although our human nature tries to convince us that selfishness fits like a glove, in truth, God has made us for something better.

Romans 15:1–7 (NIV) has instructions for this better life:

> We who are strong ought to bear with the failings of the weak and not to please ourselves. Each of us should please his neighbor for his good, to build him up. For even Christ did not please Himself but, as it is written: "The insults of those who insult you have fallen on Me." For everything that was written in the past was written to teach us, so that through endurance and the encouragement of the Scriptures we might have hope.
>
> May the God who gives endurance and encouragement give you a spirit of unity among yourselves as you follow Christ Jesus, so that with one heart and mouth you may glorify the God and Father of our Lord Jesus Christ.
>
> Accept one another, then, just as Christ accepted you, in order to bring praise to God.

Instead of asking, "What's in it for me?" my question should be, "How can I help?" Jesus modeled this unselfish attitude for us by leaving the comfort and luxury of heaven to be born in a barn, do the menial work of a carpenter, wander around for three years, and, finally, submit to torture and a horrible death on a cross. He did all this because He cared more about me than His own comfort.

Our heavenly Father encourages us to follow Jesus' example of service and humbleness, and not just because it's the right one to emulate. He knows that taking off the boots of selfishness will release us from the binding effect of self-centeredness so we can experience the freedom and joy of unity as we serve each other.

Let's ditch the boots that pinch.

Dear Jesus, thank You for Your example of unselfishness. Help me to follow in Your footsteps, leaving behind the self-centeredness that this world pursues and discovering true purpose in a life of service. In Your name. Amen.

Day Two
Wardrobe Workout

1. What is your reaction to Donald Miller's statement, "If you think about it, the human race is pretty self-absorbed. Racism might be the symptom of a greater disease" (see p. 143)?

2. Read Mark 10:35–45.

   a. What is your first response to the behavior of James and John?

b. What does their request (v. 37) reveal about human nature?

c. In verse 42, Jesus describes the behavior of the Gentiles (non-Jews). His comments about the Gentiles can be generalized to describe the natural state of humanity. How does Jesus portray the attitudes of humanity? Have things changed since He walked the earth? Give modern-day examples of the world's selfish outlook.

d. According to Jesus, if we follow Him, our attitudes and behavior will be different (v. 43–44). How will our actions contrast with those of the world?

e. Reread verse 45. Recount some other instances in Jesus' earthly ministry when He displayed acts of service (suggestion: John 13:1–17). How can you walk in His shoes today?

3. What key lesson did you learn today?

4. Write out our memory verse for this week: "This is how we know what love is: Jesus Christ laid down His life for us. And we ought to lay down our lives for our brothers" (1 John 3:16 NIV). Read a phrase, then cover it and write it. Try to do as much of the verse as you can without looking.

Day Three
◇◇◇◇◇◇◇◇◇◇◇◇◇◇◇◇
Shoes of Love

For this is the message that you have heard from the beginning,
that we should love one another.
1 John 3:11

"If the shoe fits, buy it in every color." My sister gave me a pillow embroidered with those words because she knows I love shoes. I adore sandals, loafers, and tennis shoes. I like mules, peep-toe pumps, and sling-backs.

For a time, I even liked those boots of selfishness. Because I thought they fit so well, I wore them in the color of self-centeredness, the hue of self-interest, and the shade of self-absorption. Now I know that those boots do not fit me at all, and my Savior is urging me to throw them out. He is encouraging me to be more giving and to offer more of myself instead of wondering what I can get out of life. I'm ready to exchange those well-heeled boots for flats that will help me serve and love others.

Serving others is hard. I'll admit it. I almost didn't write this chapter because, honestly, I have such a long way to go in this area. Too often, when I look down at my feet, the boots of selfishness are still there. About the only progress I have made on the road to selflessness is the recognition that I need new footwear!

What should we wear instead? Once, I heard a presentation on Christian characteristics to instill in children. The speaker made one particularly thought-provoking point. He stated that the opposite of love is not hate but selfishness. It follows, then, that the opposite of selfishness is love: not the mushy, romantic, weak-in-the-knees kind of love we see in the movies, but the self-sacrificing love we see in the life of Christ. The love of Christ does not ask, "What's in it for me?" His love is not just affection, but action. This kind of love might not be deserved or may be difficult to give. Let's wear shoes of love.

The apostle John wrote, "This is the message that you have heard from the beginning, that we should love one another" (1 John 3:11).

Yes, John, we have heard this before. The command to "love your neighbor as yourself" goes back as far as Moses, when God gave him the Law in Leviticus 19:18. And Jesus declared that the two greatest commandments are to love the Lord with all our hearts and to love our neighbors as ourselves (Luke 10:27).

For me, loving the Lord is so much easier than loving my neighbor. Although I fall short of loving God with all my heart, soul, mind, and strength (Mark 12:30), it is something I work on a lot more than on loving others. I enjoy my prayer time with the Lord, reading His Word to discover what He has to say to me, singing praises to Him in worship, and receiving Him at the altar.

I agree with what Jarrod Jones says in his book, *The Backward Life*:

> Many people (like me) can get pretty good at enjoying the vertical love, the love between them and God. But the part we get spiritual dementia about is the horizontal love—love for others. If you ask me, Christianity would be much easier if not for people. (Jones, p. 36)

Why is it so much easier to love God than people? Because God loves me first! People may not always respond in caring, compassionate ways. God is always good. People are not. God is always patient, waiting for me to come to Him. People may need me at inconvenient times.

Yet Jesus tells us without room for debate that loving others is important! Loving the Lord is to be our number one priority. But number two on Christ's must-do list is not self-fulfillment, self-esteem, or self-discovery: "You shall love the Lord your God with all your heart and with all your soul and with all your mind. This is the great and first commandment. And a second is like it: You shall love your neighbor as yourself" (Matthew 22:37–39).

1 Corinthians 13 is a miniature textbook on the subject of love. Verse 5 (NIV) reminds me that love is not "self-seeking." Love does not insist on its own way. It doesn't yell, "Me first!"

Instead, "love is patient" (v. 4). It doesn't tap its toes when someone is infringing on its time. Love doesn't push others out of the way just to get to the front of the line. It accepts interruptions as possible God-ordained appointments. Love is kind (v. 4). It treats others with respect. Love uses its best manners, even when it doesn't feel like it. It looks people in the eye and asks, "How was your day?" Love "hopes all things" (v. 7). It thinks the finest thoughts about the other person, not the worst. Love looks for exceptional qualities in her neighbors. It believes each person has the potential for greatness.

So let's wear shoes of love. Slip on shoes in the color of patience. Lace up shoes in the hue of kindness. Buckle on shoes in the shade of looking for the best in the other person. These are shoes of service in Jesus' name.

> *Dear Father, so many times when I look down at my feet, I am still wearing the boots of selfishness. I want to wear the shoes of love. Help me to make loving You and loving others numbers one and two on my life's to-do list. In Jesus' name and for His sake. Amen.*

Day Three

Wardrobe Workout

1. Below are some synonyms and antonyms for *selfish*. Prayerfully consider them and circle two or three that describe you right now.

SELFISH	*UNSELFISH*
Self-seeking	Selfless
Self-centered	Generous
Self-indulgent	Loving
Egotistical	Thoughtful
Wrapped up in one's self	Kind
Looking out for number one	Altruistic

If you circled any words in the *selfish* column, go to Jesus in prayer to receive His grace and forgiveness!

2. Read God's textbook on love: 1 Corinthians 13.

a. If you were wearing the shoes of love, what would they look like according to this chapter?

b. How can you show patience to the people in your life this week?

c. How can you show kindness this week?

d. How can you look for the best in the people you know?

3. What key lesson did you learn today?

4. Write out this week's memory verse. Try not to peek!

Day Four

Shoes of Life and Sacrifice

We know that we have passed out of death into life, because we
love the brothers. Whoever does not love abides in death. . . . By
this we know love, that He laid down His life for us, and we ought
to lay down our lives for the brothers.
1 John 3:14, 16

During my college years, I worked at a bridal salon in the summertime, alter-ing bridal gowns and bridesmaid dresses. When business was slow, the woman who owned the shop would share what was happening in her life. One day, she told us about a party she had attended. She had agonized over what to wear because she wanted to make a good impression. She finally settled on a shimmery dress that complimented her figure and a pair of high-heeled pumps that showed off her legs. Arriving fashionably late, she confidently strutted into the party on her four-inch heels, sat down, crossed her legs, and realized she had on two different shoes! They were the same style, but different colors. She certainly made a memorable impres-sion.

I often find that I am wearing two different shoes. I'm trying to wear the well-heeled boot of selfishness on one foot along with the flat shoe of love on the other. This combination is making me limp and slowing me down.

The apostle John tells me:

> We know that we have passed out of death into life, because
> we love the brothers. Whoever does not love abides in death.
> (1 John 3:14)

John is telling me that if I am not loving other people, I am not truly alive. My existence is lifeless. My limping walk is leading to a dead end, not to a vibrant life.

John also gives practical advice on loving others:

> By this we know love, that He laid down His life for us, and we
> ought to lay down our lives for the brothers. But if anyone has
> the world's goods and sees his brother in need, yet closes his

> heart against him, how does God's love abide in him? Little
> children, let us not love in word or talk but in deed and in truth.
> (1 John 3:16–18)

Part of my husband's role as pastor is to be a premarital counselor. Often, he sees young men who passionately declare their love for their fiancée by stating that they would throw themselves in front of an oncoming truck in order to save their beloved. My husband will praise their love, then ask, "If you are willing to lay down your life, are you also willing to take out the garbage? do the dishes? get up with a sick child in the middle of the night?"

We are to lay down our lives for those we love, but that does not just mean throwing ourselves in front of a truck to save them. It means laying down our time-tables, our to-do lists, or our preferences in order to give to someone, even when it's unscheduled or inconvenient or when we just don't care.

This is where loving becomes difficult. When you have children, you learn about loving even when you don't feel like it. You wake up for 2:00 a.m. feedings, rock crying babies for hours, and clean up gallons of bodily fluids.

I have tried to love my friends and the people in my church and community. I provide casseroles or banana bread to those who are ill or grieving. I contribute to the fund for hungry children in the Sudan and the parentless in Haiti. I volunteer at the school across the street. I listen when they need to talk.

But when I look at my list of good deeds, I feel that what I have done is not really laying down my life. The things I have done are not all that sacrificial. They aren't even terribly inconvenient. What does it mean when the only sacrificial thing I can remember doing in the last week is peeling potatoes, which I don't like doing, so my husband can have his favorite side dish?

Sacrificial love wears shoes of action—"in deed," as we read in 1 John 3:18—not just words. Sacrificial love is selfless: it puts others ahead of me; it submits. Love models Christ. I can ask myself each day what I can do to love my family and the people in my church sacrificially.

John continues this thought in 2 John 1:6–7:

> And this is love, that we walk according to His commandments; this
> is the commandment, just as you have heard from the beginning, so
> that you should walk in it. For many deceivers have gone out into
> the world, those who do not confess the coming of Jesus Christ in
> the flesh.

In his book *Crazy Love*, Francis Chan challenges us to go beyond being luke-warm Christians to loving like Christ:

> My suggestion as you think, make decisions, and discern how God would have you live is to ask yourself, "Is this the most loving way to do life? Am I loving my neighbor and my God by living where I live, by driving what I drive, by talking how I talk?" I urge you to consider and actually live as though each person you come into contact with is Christ. (Chan, p. 166)

I am truly alive when I wear shoes of sacrifice and walk the walk. I practice the most loving way of life by modeling Christ to everyone I know and see.

Dear Jesus Christ, too often I have tried to wear selfishness and love at the same time. May Your Spirit help me to wear the shoes of sacrifice, to learn the most loving way of life every day. Amen.

Day Four
Wardrobe Workout

1. Do you agree that loving others sacrificially can lead to a more vibrant life? Why or why not?

2. Read 3 John 1:2–4. In what ways do you walk in truth in your local congregation? in your home? in your job? in your community?

3. Now turn to 1 John 3:1–3.

   a. Where does this love come from?

   b. How do we receive it?

   c. What is our hope?

4. What key lesson did you learn today?

5. Write out this week's memory verse. No peeking!

◇◇◇◇◇◇◇◇◇◇◇◇◇
Study Styles

Asking and answering your own questions is another excellent study style. As you meditate on a passage, let your mind ponder the details and wonder how the passage speaks to your life. A good place to start is with the six questions any journalist knows: **Who? What? Where? When? Why? How?**

Read Romans 12:1–13. Invent a question or two in each category. I have given you some to get you started. Then answer the questions to the best of your ability. Discuss any problems or difficulties in the passage with your group or your pastor.

What is the theme of this passage? _____

_____

Where does true transformation take place (v. 2)? _____

_____

When can we discover God's will (v. 2)? _____

_____

Why do we serve each other (v. 5)? _____

_____

How can we live unselfishly? _____

_____

Day Five

<><><><><><><><><><><><><><><><><><><><><><><><><><>

Shoes of Grace and Purpose

*By this we shall know that we are of the truth and reassure our
heart before Him; for whenever our heart condemns us, God is
greater than our heart, and He knows everything.*
1 John 3:19–20

When I look at my well-worn boots of selfishness, I start to feel hopeless and
helpless. After all, I will never measure up to Christ's love. That's when I need to
read on in John's letter to find reassurance in God's presence.

I am not feeling very good about my own selfishness and lack of love in action.
Although I want to wear shoes of love and sacrifice, I often end up wearing the boots
of selfishness again. I may start the day with good intentions: lunches for my children
with an extra treat or note of encouragement, letting the person coming out of the
Dunkin' Donuts drive-through get in front of me in the long line of traffic, or holding the door for my co-worker as we walk into the office.

Too often, the day goes downhill from there. The boss assigns extra tasks to my
already daunting workload. Someone else takes the last pastry in the break room.
The copier breaks down—for the third time this week.

By the time I get home, I'm tired and grouchy. I slap dinner together and barely
talk through the meal. I put off my kindergartner's request to read a story: "Not
now." Hubby wants a back rub and . . . Are you kidding?

I flop into bed. In the quietness, I can finally hear my heart. "You really blew it
again. Look how you treated your family. And you call yourself a Christian."

Sound familiar?

Now what?

John says that even when my heart condemns me, God is greater than my heart.
I can go to Him for forgiveness and receive His grace. I am cleansed because of Jesus'
sacrifice for me.

"He knows everything," John says. In the Greek, this word for *knowing* means
an intimate knowledge, a complete understanding. God knows my heart. He sees my
failed good intentions. He knows my struggles and is aware of my puny opinion of
myself when I fall short. He also recognizes me as His dearly loved daughter,

baptized and redeemed by Christ. Because of Jesus, I am forgiven. Now God sees me as pure and spotless, because His grace has wiped my heart clean.

God's grace works continuously in my heart. His Holy Spirit is transforming my selfish heart to be more loving and giving. Christ in me gives me the ability to love. I cannot do it on my own. Self-absorption, self-indulgence, and even self-addiction are my usual wardrobe choices. It is only through Christ's love that I have any love to give, and any capability to think beyond my own needs and wants, any ability to choose sacrifice over selfishness. Thank God for His gift of limitless grace!

When I revert to my usual footwear of selfishness, God in His Word shows me that this is not the path to a life of joy: "Everyone who has left houses or brothers or sisters or father or mother or children or lands, for My name's sake, will receive a hundredfold and will inherit eternal life" (Matthew 19:29). We are more alive when we give ourselves away. The Holy Spirit gives me the strength to choose the shoes of love instead.

So this is where I begin: through God's grace and love working in my heart, I will live life as though it were meant to be given away. In *The Backward Life*, Jarrod Jones writes about this way of life as the true path to purpose and fulfillment:

> Jesus' answer is not the love of self but the love for God and love
> for others. This is the key to freedom, the key to joy, the key to ful-
> fillment, the key to purpose. The key to life is that we're not made
> for "self," we're made for God—and made to give away our lives to
> other people. (Jones, p. 22)

Satan, in the guise of the world around us, tries to tell us that our reason for living is self-actualization, self-fulfillment, and self-esteem. But we are not of the world (John 15:19). Our Lord Jesus tells us that our function is to love Him and love others, and as we live out that purpose, we will experience genuine fulfillment. It is when we give ourselves away as a manifestation of Jesus' love for us that we obtain our real life.

Join me in throwing out the uncomfortable boots of selfishness and putting on the shoes that we are designed to wear: shoes of love, sacrifice, and grace. Then we will find the footwear that fits divinely: shoes of life and purpose.

> *Thank You, Father, that You know my heart. You see my good in-*
> *tentions and my failures. Because of Jesus, You also see my heart*
> *pure and clean. Give me the strength to choose love over selfish-*

ness. Help me to discover this key to true fulfillment. In Jesus'
name. Amen.

Day Five
◇◇◇◇◇◇◇◇◇◇◇◇◇◇◇◇◇◇◇◇◇◇
Wardrobe Workout

1. What is your reaction to the words, "God is greater than our heart, and He knows everything" (1 John 3:20)?

2. What key lesson did you learn today?

3. Write 1 John 3:16 NIV from memory.

Meaningful Makeover

How can we boot out the boots of selfishness and wear the shoes of love instead?

What does love look like in your life? How can you make small sacrifices for your family, friends, community, and world to demonstrate your love? Is God calling you to any big sacrifices? Record your thoughts here.

Meditate on these words from Scripture: "This is how we know what love is: Jesus Christ laid down His life for us. And we ought to lay down our lives for our brothers" (1 John 3:16 NIV).

How can you lay down your sacrificial love for the following:

Family

Friends

Community

World

Circle one and resolve to implement it this week!

Remember to bring your boots to your group's meeting!

WEEK SEVEN

BITTERNESS—Banish This Sweater

Memory Verse

Put on then, as God's chosen ones, holy and beloved, compassionate hearts, kindness, humility, meekness, and patience, bearing with one another and, if one has a complaint against another, forgiving each other; as the Lord has forgiven you, so you also must forgive.

Colossians 3:12–13

Day One

◇◇

The Comfortable Bitterness Sweater

*Let all bitterness and wrath and anger and clamor and slander be
put away from you, along with all malice. Be kind to one another,
tenderhearted, forgiving one another, as God in Christ forgave you.*
Ephesians 4:31–32

Bitterness is a common material we wear when we've been hurt. And who
hasn't been hurt? Family members offend us. Friends ignore us. Co-workers speak
wounding words. People we've trusted tell our secrets. Someone else gets the promo-
tion. Spouses are unfaithful.

That's when we grab the bitterness sweater. Its warm, thick knit comforts us
against the chill from the world. We store up all those angry feelings, playing them
over and over in our minds. Every time we think of the situation, we are aware of the
ache in our heart. We pull that sweater tighter around us, not willing to let go of our
resentment.

Sometimes we seek the comfort of bitterness because of a serious offense, such
as a spouse's adulterous affair. But we may also grab onto resentment because of a
minor fault, like someone's failure to send us a thank you note. Sometimes anger
builds over a misunderstanding and grows over time.

Bitterness is essentially stored anger. It is bottled rage, kept under pressure in
our minds. Resentment and anger are best dealt with quickly, but sometimes we
disregard the sting in our hearts, or perhaps we nurse the ache, thinking this will also
cause the other person equal discomfort or even agony. Occasionally, we latch onto
bitterness because of a situation we view as unfair, and we spread our antagonism to
all involved.

My senior year in high school was my most shameful period of bitterness. It
didn't start out that way. I was enjoying a fantastic finale to my high school career.
Classes were going well. I participated in band, choir, and orchestra with two of the
most amazing people ever: Deb and Barb. Our friendship was orchestrated through
our love of music, but it was also composed of shared dreams and laughter.

As the school year wound down, I kept my eye on my goal: maintaining my
grade point average so I could be one of the graduation speakers. By my calculations,

I was sure I had one of the two spots secured. However, just as I was certain of my position, I heard the news that I was not chosen for the honor. "Yes, your grade point was highest," I was told, "but this year we decided to take extracurricular activities into consideration as well. We've chosen Deb."

Instead of feeling joy for my friend, I felt only anger. Yes, Deb was more talented and more active in school activities, but I had concentrated on my grades to achieve my goal. Then the rules were changed, and I was left out. It wasn't fair.

To my disgrace, I did not let go of my disappointment or my anger at those who had made the decision. I even let that resentment boil over to Deb. Instead of what should have been an exciting, enjoyable final season of a great senior year, I stubbornly avoided Deb, fumed about the graduation ceremony, and ruminated about the unfairness of it all. I even secretly hoped her speech would be a flop, but instead it was entertaining, moving, and inspiring.

My bitterness sweater comforted me with my thoughts of resentment, my obsession with the situation, and my animosity toward Deb. I wore it a long time before I gave it up.

This week, we will examine the story of an Old Testament man who initially comforted himself with bitterness. Many of you will recall the story of Joseph (found in Genesis 37–50). You could certainly say he had reason for bitterness. His own brothers turned on him, first plotting to kill him, then relenting, mercifully selling him into slavery. He endured a long journey through the desert, chained, on foot, and treated like baggage. Upon arriving in Egypt, he spent thirteen years as a slave and prisoner. And you thought your siblings were brutal!

Through God's sovereignty, Joseph's circumstances changed while he was in prison. Pharaoh had some disturbing dreams, which no one could interpret. The royal cupbearer remembered that two years earlier, Joseph had interpreted a dream for him. Now the cupbearer reported this incident to the head of the land. Pharaoh sent for Joseph, who interpreted the dreams as God revealed. The dreams indicated that there would be seven years of plenty followed by seven years of famine. Joseph suggested that Pharaoh appoint someone to store up grain during the years of abundance to be used during the years of famine. Pharaoh was dutifully impressed and told Joseph, "You're the man."

In this way, Joseph became the second-most important official in the greatest superpower of the day. He led Egypt in the task of storing enough grain for seven years. Then, just as God had told him, the famine hit. This famine affected not only Egypt, but also Canaan, where Joseph's family was still living.

Meanwhile, Joseph's brothers heard that there was grain available in Egypt, so they traveled to obtain some for their families. When they arrived, they were ushered into the presence of the vice-president of Egypt: Joseph. Although they did not recognize him, he knew them, and "he treated them like strangers and spoke roughly to them" (Genesis 42:7). Joseph accused them of being spies and even put one of the brothers in prison.

Why would Joseph do that? Perhaps Joseph was storing up more than grain. Perhaps he wanted his brothers to experience some of the hurt, rejection, and pain they had inflicted on him. He was not yet ready to let go of his resentment.

Bitterness fuels anger for years. Bitterness does not let go of the hurt. Bitterness wishes pain on those who inflicted our pain. Somehow we think that unforgiveness will nurture our hurt feelings. Our stored anger will be a protective shield around our tender hearts. Our bitterness sweater will comfort our minds.

But Jesus offers us a new style. He doesn't want us to continue in the fashion of unforgiveness and anger. He will help us realize that the bitterness sweater is actually irritating our spirits, not comforting them. Christ can unravel our bitterness and enable us to choose a sweater of forgiveness. He modeled this garment Himself, forgiving our sins and mistakes when He bore them to the cross on our behalf. At His Table, He wraps us in a fresh, new garment, one that frees our restricted, resentful souls and comforts as nothing else can.

Savior, forgive me for when I have wrapped bitterness around my soul and not forgiven others, even though You have forgiven me. Help me to choose forgiveness, following Your example. In Your name. Amen.

Day One
Wardrobe Workout

1. Which sweater are you most likely to wear: the warm-but-scratchy bitterness sweater or the softer-than-cashmere forgiveness sweater? Sort through your wardrobe to find a sweater that symbolizes your usual reaction toward people who offend you. Bring your sweater to your group meeting.

2. Why do you think bitterness is such a natural reaction when we've been hurt?

3. Bitterness is stored anger. How do you deal with anger? Write out the following verses and mark on the scale where you see your usual response to anger.

1 Corinthians 13:4–5 _____

_____

●——●

I tend to keep score.   **I tend to let minor**   **I remember every slight.**
                                   faults slide.

Ephesians 4:26 _____

_____

●——●

I tend to fume over hurtful situations without   **I tend to take care of issues quickly.**
settling them with the other person.

Romans 12:19 _____

_____

●——●

When angered, I dwell on ways   **When angered, I tend to leave the**
to get even.   **problem in God's hands.**

4. What key lesson did you learn today?

5. Our memory verse for this week is Colossians 3:12–13: "Put on then, as God's chosen ones, holy and beloved, compassionate hearts, kindness, humility, meekness, and patience, bearing with one another and, if one has a complaint against another, forgiving each other; as the Lord has forgiven you, so you also must forgive." To help you memorize this passage, write it out in the space below.

Day Two

◇◇◇

The Uncomfortable Bitterness Sweater

*For if you forgive others their trespasses, your heavenly Father will
also forgive you, but if you do not forgive others their trespasses,
neither will your Father forgive your trespasses.*
Matthew 6:14–15

When we first pull on the bitterness sweater, it feels so comfortable. It deceptively warms our emotions as we brood on our hurt feelings and hope for some of the same for the offender.

But eventually, bitterness inflicts consequences in our lives. The bitterness sweater is an irritant to our body, mind, and spirit; it affects our health, relationships, and spiritual well-being. That warm-but-scratchy sweater of stored anger can rub away our emotional health, chafe our hearts, and aggravate our spirits.

Studies show that holding on to resentment is bad for our physical well-being. In an article for MentalHealth.net, Harry Mills, PhD, writes that medical science clearly shows a negative impact on heart health when we hold on to anger. In addition, research bears out that chronic aggression and anger can raise the risk of deadly heart disease fivefold (Mills, "Health Costs of Anger," MentalHealth.net). A 2004 article in *Newsweek* reported that feelings of anger and unforgivingness can also impair our immune systems, affect memory capacity, and cause back pain (Jordana Lewis and Jerry Adler, "Forgive and Let Live," *Newsweek* [October 4, 2004], p. 52).

Resentment will not only affect our bodies but it will also inflame our souls. At first it feels warm and comfortable, but as we persist in it, we will feel miserable. Initially, I felt justified in my anger about the unfairness of the graduation speech. I thought the powers that be had changed the rules without letting me know. Unfortunately, my persistent bitterness spoiled my enjoyment of the commencement ceremony and ruined my friendship with Deb.

Joseph, too, felt agony and distress. Even as he was putting one brother in jail and falsely accusing the others of spying, Joseph had to turn away from his brothers and weep. Revenge was not as sweet as he thought it would be. Joseph sent his family away without revealing himself to them. By doing so, he caused them to feel anxious and guilt-ridden, and he delayed his reconciliation with them.

My friend Gail experienced the negative effects of bitterness. One of Gail's trusted friends betrayed her, and the betrayal destroyed the friendship. The unfaithfulness wounded her spirit, and Gail noticed that bitterness was creeping into her life. She wrapped a little resentment around her emotions and tried to ignore her wounded heart. Eventually, Gail noticed that the anger and hurt that she stored in her heart began to bleed into her other relationships. Because Gail was slow to deal with her injured feelings, she was hesitant to trust other people.

Then God spoke to Gail through the words of Psalm 20:7, "Some trust in chariots and some in horses, but we trust in the name of the Lord our God." She realized that God alone is perfectly trustworthy. "Some trust in chariots and some in horses." Some trust in family members. Some trust in friends. All of these can fail us. But if we "trust in the name of the Lord our God," He will never disappoint us, never disillusion us, and never let us down.

Gail learned that in order to have joy, she had to let go of her bitterness and hang on to the only One worthy of complete trust. Exchanging her sweater of resentment for Christ's garment of grace healed her heart.

The sweater of bitterness will also scratch our spirits, affecting our relationship with God. Jesus taught that the forgiveness we receive is tied to the forgiveness we extend:

> For if you forgive others their trespasses, your heavenly Father will
> also forgive you, but if you do not forgive others their trespasses,
> neither will your Father forgive your trespasses. (Matthew 6:14–15)

When we recognize that we are all sinners requiring God's mercy and forgiveness, we are more willing to extend the grace we have received to others. On the other hand, if we feel that we deserve God's grace and others don't, our bitterness grows and we build a wall around us, cutting us off from God's grace. In her book *Choosing Forgiveness*, Nancy Leigh DeMoss writes, "When we refuse to forgive, something is blocked in our relationship with the Father" (DeMoss, p. 70).

The bitterness sweater does not allow us to feel God's touch of mercy. Resentment distances us from God. When we allow God to remove the anger, when we extend the forgiveness that Jesus offers to those who have hurt us, then we, too, can experience God's grace. The itchy sweater of bitterness disappears and we are in God's embrace, forgiven and restored. "For all have sinned and fall short of the glory of God," St. Paul tells us, "and are justified by His grace as a gift, through the redemption that is in Christ Jesus" (Romans 3:23–24).

It's time to eliminate the warm-but-scratchy bitterness sweater from our wardrobes. It promises false comfort; its real effect is to irritate our health, relationships, and connection to God. Forgiveness frees us to enjoy the life God gives us and to preserve the friendships He blesses us with. As we offer His grace to others, we encounter anew God's merciful touch.

God of grace, at times resentment and anger have harmed my life.
Help me to let go of bitterness. Enable me to forgive others freely,
so that I may receive Your grace. In Jesus' name and for His sake.
Amen.

Day Two
Wardrobe Workout

1. Do you agree that bitterness can affect our bodies and souls? When have you experienced the negative effects of bitterness?

2. Read Matthew 18:21–35.

   a. In verse 21, Peter asks Jesus how many times he should forgive his brother. What do you think his question says about human nature?

   b. Jesus tells Peter that he should forgive "seventy times seven" times (some versions say seventy-seven times). What basic principle about forgiveness do you think Jesus teaches here?

   c. The unmerciful servant owed the master ten thousand talents—roughly two hundred thousand years' wages! What does this huge debt represent in our lives? How does this knowledge change the way you view God's gift of forgiveness to you?

   d. The fellow servant owed one hundred denarii, or one hundred days' wages. That's nothing to sneeze at, but it's minuscule compared to the first servant's debt. Looking at times in your life when forgiveness has been difficult, why do you think the unmerciful servant refused to cancel the debt?

   e. What did the master call the unmerciful servant (v. 32)? What does this tell you about God's view on withholding forgiveness?

   f. Read the fate of the unmerciful servant (v. 34). What happens to us when we hang on to bitterness?

g. Describe the lesson you learned from Jesus' story. How can you use that lesson this week?

3. What key lesson did you learn this week?

4. Write out our memory verse for this week: "Put on then, as God's chosen ones, holy and beloved, compassionate hearts, kindness, humility, meekness, and patience, bearing with one another and, if one has a complaint against another, forgiving each other; as the Lord has forgiven you, so you also must forgive" (Colossians 3:12–13). Write it out phrase by phrase, trying to do as much of it as you can by memory.

Day Three

⟡⟡⟡⟡⟡⟡⟡⟡⟡⟡⟡⟡⟡⟡⟡⟡⟡⟡⟡⟡⟡

The Choice of Forgiveness

*And whenever you stand praying, forgive, if you have anything
against anyone, so that your Father also who is in heaven may
forgive you your trespasses.*
Mark 11:25

Forgiveness begins with a choice. At first, it may seem easier to hang on to bitterness. Forgiveness may seem too high a price to pay. Bitterness advertises itself as a bargain; it's so much easier to come by than forgiveness. Then we realize that bitterness actually costs us more in terms of health and peace of mind. When we realize that we are only punishing ourselves rather than the offender, we can turn to the Father to help us make the decision to forgive.

Back in high school, I grabbed on to that bitterness sweater and didn't let go for a long time. I couldn't seem to forgive the school officials that made the unfair decision. Irrationally, I also blamed Deb in her role. After high school, Deb and I parted ways. A couple of years later, we ended up at the same college. When I saw her, I realized how foolish I had been. I let go of my anger toward the original decision-makers and toward my friend. I was eventually able to confess my wrong attitude to Deb and receive her forgiveness.

Joseph also made the choice to forgive his brothers for the misery that they had brought into his life. Although I think he initially wanted to make them suffer a little, when they came to Egypt for food a second time, Joseph forgave them. He called the brothers to his home and drew them close. Revealing himself as Joseph, he said, "Do not be distressed or angry with yourselves because you sold me here" (Genesis 45:5). Joseph could have used his authority to throw them all into prison, but instead he embraced them. "He kissed all his brothers and wept upon them" (v. 15). Joseph's choice to forgive his brothers restored the relationship between them.

Certainly, we can come up with many reasons to continue in unforgiveness. It's difficult to let go of our anger. We don't think the offender deserves mercy. Wallowing in bitterness makes us feel as if we're doing something to punish the person that hurt us. We feel justified.

The Bible tells us otherwise:

See to it that no one fails to obtain the grace of God; that no "root
of bitterness" springs up and causes trouble, and by it many become
defiled. (Hebrews 12:15)

Bitterness is a poison. Although we may think we are giving the toxin to the
offender through our continued resentment, the poison is actually entering our own
souls. The venom pollutes our lives with unnecessary trouble and corruption. It
blinds us to the grace of God.

Forgiveness does not originate with an emotion but with a resolve to follow
Christ. When Jesus was instructing His disciples about prayer, He told them, "And
whenever you stand praying, forgive, if you have anything against anyone, so that
your Father also who is in heaven may forgive you your trespasses" (Mark 11:25).
Did Jesus say, "When you feel like forgiving the person who hurt you, forgive him,"
or "If the rat who broke your heart is truly sorry, let him off the hook," or "After the
mafia has broken all his bones to even the score, then forgive him"?

No. Jesus teaches us that whenever we are holding something against anyone,
we are to forgive. In fact, He modeled this choice to forgive even when He was
hurting. As men jammed sharp thorns into His skull, pounded nails into His hands
and feet, and suspended Him on a cross, Jesus prayed, "Father, forgive them, for they
know not what they do" (Luke 23:34). He did not allow pain to cripple His ability to
forgive.

Our feelings are changeable and unpredictable, but God's ways never change.
Because our feelings are unreliable and affected by our circumstances, there will be
many times when they do not line up with God's will. We need to choose which way
we will follow.

Our emotions often prevent us from extending forgiveness because we feel that
the person who hurt us does not deserve to be forgiven. Sometimes the offender
does not even realize the harm she has done. She is going on with her life, while we
are stuck in a rerun of painful events. Or perhaps the person who hurt us is not one
bit repentant. She refuses to admit she is at fault and may even continue the wounding behavior.

The Roman soldiers who crucified Jesus were guilty of a terrible crime. Execut-
ing an innocent man was bad enough, but crucifying the Son of God should have
deserved the most severe punishment. Still, Jesus asked the Father to forgive them.
He forgave those who do not deserve forgiveness.

Following our emotions is a natural choice, but in the end, we choose forgiveness because the Lord God commands it. By the gifts of the Holy Spirit, He empow-

ers us to do so. We choose forgiveness because we have been given grace and mercy. We choose to forgive because to continue in bitterness means death to our souls.

Author of forgiveness, thank You for Your example of mercy in spite of pain. Help me to follow Your Word instead of my feelings. Help me to choose to forgive. Amen.

Day Three
Wardrobe Workout

1. Today we read, "Forgiveness does not originate with an emotion, but with a resolve to follow Christ." Is this a new concept to you? How can it help you the next time someone offends you?

2. The Bible instructs us to "Forgive as the Lord forgave you" (Colossians 3:13 NIV). Discover some characteristics of God's forgiveness.

   Job 14:16–17

   Psalm 103:11–12

   Isaiah 43:25

Can you think of some practical ways to put these principles of forgiveness to work in your life?

3. What key lesson did you learn this week?

4. Write out this week's memory verse. Try not to peek.

Day Four

Unraveling Bitterness

But Joseph said to them, "Do not fear, for am I in the place of God? As for you, you meant evil against me, but God meant it for good, to bring it about that many people should be kept alive, as they are today."
Genesis 50:19–20

When life makes us want to clutch that bitterness sweater and pull it closer around us, we may ask, "Where is God in this hurt?"

God is with us in the pain, offering not only the choice but also the grace to forgive. As He works in our hearts, the Holy Spirit opens our eyes to a new style: freedom from resentment. Just as with any other new fashion, we may resist the change at first. Eventually, we recognize the wisdom of God's design, yet it appears just out of reach. The price seems too costly. It is then that God freely offers His grace so that we can offer it to others. Nancy Leigh DeMoss writes:

> When we get hurt, no matter how serious the offense or how deep the wound, God has grace available to help us deal with the offense and forgive the offender. At that point, we have one of two choices. We can acknowledge our need and humbly reach out to Him for His grace to forgive and release the offender. Or we can resist Him, fail to receive His grace, and hold on to the hurt. (DeMoss, p. 75)

As we receive the garment of forgiveness, Jesus unravels our bitterness and knits a new luxurious pattern for our lives.

God is with us when we hurt, recording our tears, feeling our pain, and using that very hurt to transform our lives. There are times in our lives when we will be required to wear garments of heartache and agony. Our divine Designer does not hand these out haphazardly, however. We can be sure that every garment of loss and hurt that God allows into our lives has been tenderly measured to fit into His ultimate plan for our lives.

As Joseph's father neared death, Joseph's brothers got a little nervous. What if Joseph were merely waiting for Papa to pass on before he unleashed a little payback? The brothers nervously told him, "Uh, Joseph? Dad wanted us to tell you something. He wants you to forget about the time we plotted to kill you. Oh, and the time we threw you into a pit too. And, if you wouldn't mind, the time we sold you off to some slave traders as well."

Joseph graciously reassured them of his forgiveness: "But Joseph said to them, 'Do not fear, for am I in the place of God? As for you, you meant evil against me, but God meant it for good, to bring it about that many people should be kept alive, as they are today' " (Genesis 50:19–20). Joseph recognized that God had allowed his brothers to put him through his trials. The almighty, all-knowing Sovereign used each painful circumstance not only for Joseph's benefit but also to help many others.

It is often hard to see how anything good can come out of the pain we've experienced. When my friend Rebecca discovered that her husband was having an affair, she was devastated. Something she held sacred was desecrated. She thought about abandoning the marriage, but then she decided to see if it could be saved. As she wrestled with forgiveness and trust, she also struggled to find a positive purpose in what she had endured.

Rebecca brought this struggle to the counseling sessions she and her husband attended. The counselor pointed out that the benefits of the situation might not have been for her but for her husband. It was a light bulb moment for Rebecca. She could see a positive change in her husband. He was truly repentant. He admitted that he had gotten him into such serious sin because he ignored his conscience and didn't listen to God. Now Rebecca could see that he sought God and actively strove to hear God's voice. Before, her husband had a simple knowledge of faith; now he had a real relationship with his Savior.

It may be difficult to see how anything beneficial could be salvaged from a shattered marriage, what possible good could come out of an undeserved rebuke, or how something positive could be gleaned from a betrayal of friendship. Although people may harm us, God can turn it to good. The benefits may not be readily apparent, but God allows those painful times to bring about eternal benefits. We may not understand His purpose on this side of heaven, but we can trust in God's ability to transform absolute anguish into abundant blessing.

Remember, our heavenly Father is present with us. Jesus comes to us in His body and blood and refashions us so that we are ready to receive His strength and grace to forgive. He wants to unravel our bitterness and make the alterations necessary to transform our pain into purpose.

God of purpose, I know that You allow nothing in my life that does not have an eternal objective. Unravel my bitterness. Enable me to see Your intentions for good even in the painful times. In Jesus' name. Amen.

Day Four
Wardrobe Workout

1. When you experience pain or heartache, how can it help to know that God has carefully fit and measured every event in your life to suit His plan for your life?

2. How is God refashioning bitterness in your life?

3. Read 2 Timothy 1:8–10. St. Paul wrote this letter to encourage Timothy in his work. What does this verse say to you about your daily life in Christ?

4. What key lesson did you learn today?

5. Write out the memory verse for this week. No peeking!

◇◇◇◇◇◇◇◇◇◇◇◇◇◇
Study Styles

Examining a passage of the Bible in several different translations can help us to understand the passage better because each version will translate the original Greek or Hebrew words in a slightly different way. Each version can highlight a nuance of the same idea, and when we see them together, we gain new insight.

Look up Colossians 3:13 in several versions of the Bible. If you don't own numerous translations, go to www.BibleGateway.com and use the passage lookup feature available there. Write out each version and underline a phrase or word in each version that best helps you to understand the passage.

Version:

Version:

Version:

Now rewrite Colossians 3:13 using your new understanding and perhaps your underlined words and phrases.

Day Five

The Sweater of Forgiveness

Whoever covers an offense seeks love,
but he who repeats a matter separates close friends.
Proverbs 17:9

Which would you rather wear, a scratchy woolen sweater or a luxuriously soft cashmere sweater? As we end this week's study, we're ready to exchange the irritating bitterness sweater for the velvety, softer-than-cashmere sweater of forgiveness. Stored anger chafes our souls and erases our joy. Resentment continues to rub those past hurts into our minds and memories. Forgiveness relieves the abrasive effects of anger and softens our hearts.

When we make the choice to forgive, God will enable us to do so. He gives us the grace to let go of anger and resentment. Although the effects of being hurt may never totally disappear, forgiveness conceals it with love. Proverbs 17:9 tells us, "Whoever covers an offense seeks love." How can we cover up an offense?

First of all, we cover the offense by refusing to repeat the matter. We do not bring up the hurtful situation every time we see the offender. Nor do we continually discuss the problem with other friends and family members. Constantly talking about the offense will only amplify it, not erase it from our life.

Second, we cover the offense in our mind. With determination, we refuse to brood on the error or hold on to the injustice. Instead, we choose to focus on something positive about the other person or discover something we can learn from the situation. When we fasten our thoughts on what is wrong, we continue to wear that bitterness sweater. Of course, some monumental hurts will benefit from wise Christian counseling. I am not suggesting that forgiveness is always an easy process. But when we let go of the hurt through counseling and refuse to allow the pain to dominate our thoughts, we experience the freedom of forgiveness.

Although Rebecca's marriage is healing, she admits that she still struggles with anger and resentment. Painful memories appear unpredictably, set off by something in the house or on the computer. Rebecca said, "I get overwhelmed by these feelings and I have to put them somewhere in order to function. I do not want to keep them or store them or manage them." In order to deal with them, she mentally visualizes putting the pain away. She reminds herself that the infidelity is in the past and that if she is to move on with her life, she has to leave it there. When the hurtful memories pop up, she pictures a box labeled "The Past" and imagines putting her thoughts in the box, then fastening the lid. Rebecca covers the thoughts of resentment with the lid of the past.

Third, we diligently cover the offense with God's Word.

God has forgiven us and wants us to forgive others:

> Put on then, as God's chosen ones, holy and beloved, compassionate hearts, kindness, humility, meekness, and patience, bearing with one another and, if one has a complaint against another, forgiving each other; as the Lord has forgiven you, so you also must forgive. (Colossians 3:12–13)

Unforgivingness will harm our relationship with God:

> And whenever you stand praying, forgive, if you have anything against anyone, so that your Father also who is in heaven may forgive you your trespasses. (Mark 11:25)

Bitterness is a poison:

> See to it that no one fails to obtain the grace of God; that no "root of bitterness" springs up and causes trouble, and by it many become defiled. (Hebrews 12:15)

God will bring about justice:

> Beloved, never avenge yourselves, but leave it to the wrath of God,
> for it is written, "Vengeance is mine, I will repay, says the Lord."
> (Romans 12:19)

God can bring good out of terrible circumstances:

> And we know that for those who love God all things work
> together for good, for those who are called according to His purpose.
> (Romans 8:28)

God promises to be with you even in the pain:

> Be content with what you have, for He has said, "I will never leave
> you nor forsake you." (Hebrews 13:5)

Forgiveness is part of our new wardrobe:

> Let all bitterness and wrath and anger and clamor and slander be
> put away from you, along with all malice. Be kind to one another,
> tenderhearted, forgiving one another, as God in Christ forgave you.
> (Ephesians 4:31–32)

As you use God's Word to conceal and obscure the bitter thoughts, they lose their grip on you. Whenever resentment threatens to take over your mind, defeat it with Scripture. The sweater of forgiveness is knit with God's truth.

Fourth, we cover the offense with prayer. Jesus said, "Love your enemies and pray for those who persecute you" (Matthew 5:44). He told His disciples that this approach would show the world that they were different: that they were children of God. When we pray for those who harm us, we demonstrate God's love.

Prayer changes the situation. Even if the offender we pray for does not alter her behavior, we are transformed. It is very difficult to stay bitter toward people when we are consistently lifting them up in prayer.

Fifth and finally, we kneel at the Lord's Table and receive the forgiveness that Jesus freely gives us. When we confess our own sins and are absolved of them, when we hear the words "shed [for you] for the forgiveness of your sins" (*LSB*, p. 164) we can be confident that we are strengthened in faith. We can, therefore, go forward "in fervent love toward one another" (*LSB*, p. 166). Praise be to God!

God is helping you take off your bitterness sweater. He wants to unravel all the negative emotions that are tying you in knots, affecting your well-being and your relationship with the Giver of grace. He is ready to slide the soft sweater of forgiveness onto your shoulders and help you to be a conduit of that forgiveness to others in your life. In doing so, you will not only be releasing the offender but also yourself. God will bring purpose to your pain and allow you to move forward in your life as you cover over the hurt with His love.

> *Giver of grace, take the bitterness from my heart and cover it with love. Untangle my thoughts of anger and help me to leave them in the past. Make me a conduit of Your grace to the people in my life. Amen.*

Day Five
◇◇◇◇◇◇◇◇◇◇◇◇◇◇◇◇◇◇◇◇◇◇
Wardrobe Workout

1. Name the five ways to cover an offense discussed in today's chapter. Which one will be most useful to you?

2. Read a setting of "Confession and Absolution" in a hymnal. Do you have unresolved conflicts in your life? If so, think of one person toward whom you harbor bitterness. How can you take the first step toward reconciliation with that person?

3. What key lesson did you learn today?

4. Write out Colossians 3:12–13 from memory.

Meaningful Makeover

It's time to take off the bitterness sweater. Spend some time in prayer and ask God to reveal if there is anyone whom you need to forgive. Perhaps a name immediately came to mind when you began reading this chapter. Or perhaps the feelings are deeply buried.

On a sheet of paper, write the name of the person and his or her offense using a blue marker or crayon. Draw the outline of a sweater around the words on the paper.

Now go to the Lord and pray:

> *"Lord, I choose to forgive (name). Because of Your grace to me, I will pass grace on to them. Give me Your strength and love to cover over their offense and then let it go. Because I want to be free, I choose not to dwell on the offense any longer. I do forgive."*

Now use your blue marker or crayon to color in the sweater on the paper, covering over the offense. You might even want to put the paper through the shredder or burn it in an ashtray to symbolize erasing it from your life.

This process will be very difficult for some. Many women have sustained abuse, unfaithfulness, and untold hurts. Remember, Jesus will give the strength to forgive. As we do, He will release us from the prison of bitterness.

During your small group discussion, share your forgiveness stories if you are so inclined. Some small group participants may find added release by telling their whole stories, while others may leave out details and simply tell the effect of shedding their bitterness sweaters. Remind one another to seek safe Christian counsel for problems that remain overwhelming.

Remember to bring your sweater to your group's meeting!

WEEK EIGHT

LOOK IN THE MIRROR— A New You

Memory Verse

And we, who with unveiled faces all reflect the Lord's glory, are being transformed into His likeness with ever-increasing glory, which comes from the Lord, who is the Spirit.

2 Corinthians 3:18 NIV

Day One
◇◇◇◇◇◇◇◇◇◇◇◇◇
God's Mirror

*Anyone who listens to the word but does not do what it says is like
a man who looks at his face in a mirror and, after looking at himself, goes away and immediately forgets what he looks like.*
James 1:23–24 NIV

Are you ready to look in the mirror? We have reached the end of this phase of
our spiritual makeover. We have ditched the field marshal uniform of control, the
heavy purse of worry, and the prom dress of pride. Envy-green outfits, boots of selfishness, and bitterness sweaters are in the garbage can. We can expect to see a change
in our spiritual looking-glass. What will we see?

Recently, my daughter sent me a sweet picture of my one-year-old grandson. In
the photo, he has just discovered his reflection in a full-length mirror and is giving
himself a great big smooch. Adorable!

Most of us, however, are not that enamored of our reflection. Even as a young
girl, I didn't always like what I saw in the mirror. I blame it on the hairstyles. In
kindergarten, you would have thought I was trying to impersonate a thirty-year-old.
My hair was done just like my mom's: cut to a length of three inches from my scalp,
set in rollers, and fluffed for that lovely bouffant look. Second grade was the year of
the pixie cut. Remember those short 'dos? My mother tried to improve on the style
by attempting to curl my two-inch-long hair, and I ended up with half-curls sticking
up from my head like antennae! And fourth grade? Well, let me just say that was the
year I looked like I was imitating Shirley Temple. Then came the teen years. Who
wants to look at zits and braces? I spent hours at the mirror, trying to copy Farrah
Fawcett's mane, master the art of makeup, and cover those pimples. Now that those
years are behind me, little cracks keep appearing in my reflection—ooh, wait; those
are wrinkles!

Sometimes the mirror is deceiving. At times, when I catch my reflection in the
black glass of my microwave, for example, I stop and stare. The convex glass distorts
my reflection, amplifying the part of my body that doesn't need any widening: my
hips! (No hot fudge brownie for me.)

Satan and the world around us often act like those distorted mirrors. Satan likes to tell us lies: "You're not good enough." "Why do you think you can do that?" "Nobody likes you anyway." Then the world holds up other false mirrors. "You don't measure up if you're not as rich as Oprah, as famous as Angelina Jolie, or as gifted as Venus Williams." God knows exactly what we're up against, and He encourages us:

See that no one leads you astray. (Matthew 24:4)

Let no one deceive you with empty words. (Ephesians 5:6)

See to it that no one takes you captive by philosophy and empty deceit, according to human tradition, according to the elemental spirits of the world, and not according to Christ. (Colossians 2:8)

Avoid the irreverent babble and contradictions of what is falsely called "knowledge." (1 Timothy 6:20)

Avoid irreverent babble, for it will lead people into more and more ungodliness. (2 Timothy 2:16)

As obedient children, do not be conformed to the passions of your former ignorance. (1 Peter 1:14)

There are many other such passages. But Satan is insidious, and our culture is full of mirrors. Magazines such as *Glamour, Vogue,* and *Elle* compel us to reflect the models on their pages. I know I have succumbed to the subtle pressure to mirror their images. I may feel like a failure if my kitchen does not look like one in *Better Homes and Gardens*. The cover of *Shape* magazine stares at me from the grocery check-out lane and screams, "Loser," because my abs and biceps certainly do not match those of the model on the cover. I feel defeated if I can't find or can't afford the perfect pair of jeans touted in *More*.

It's easy to become focused on the mirrors of our culture, spending too much time and money trying to emulate the standards of wealth, success, and beauty that we see in the media.

What mirror are we to look at? James 1:22–25 (NIV) tells us:

Do not merely listen to the word, and so deceive yourselves. Do what it says. Anyone who listens to the word but does not do what

it says is like a man who looks at his face in a mirror and, after looking at himself, goes away and immediately forgets what he looks
like. But the man who looks intently into the perfect law that gives
freedom, and continues to do this, not forgetting what he has heard,
but doing it—he will be blessed in what he does.

The distorted mirror of the world will not give us a true picture of ourselves.
It reflects the physical world: appearance, wealth, and fame. It doesn't reflect what
truly matters: the well-being of our souls. But God's Word is a perfect mirror not
only in the sense that it is without flaws but also in the sense that it is complete. It
will reflect the total person, including the soul.

God's mirror is trustworthy. It is not like the glass on the microwave, giving a
false impression. God's mirror reflects who we really are. Sometimes this image is
not pretty, because it shows us behaviors that need to change. Nevertheless, we are
to look carefully into the mirror of God's perfect Law and act on what we see there.
If I looked in the mirror before a job interview and saw a piece of spinach between
my teeth but did nothing about it, what good did it do to look in the mirror? One of
the purposes of God's Law is to show us our sin and our need, therefore, for a Savior
from that sin. We need to look into God's Word, recognize what it shows us about
ourselves and about our need for Christ, and allow Him to change our lives.

The mirror of God's Word also tells us who we are in Christ: the Father's
chosen child, Jesus' friend, God's workmanship, not condemned but redeemed and
forgiven. The Catechism reminds us, "Since Christ was our substitute before God,
our Savior's perfect keeping of the Law is part of His saving work for us, and because
of Him we are considered righteous before God" (*Luther's Small Catechism with
Explanation*, Question 43).

When we use God's mirror, our lives are blessed.

*Father in heaven, I thank You for providing a perfect mirror in
Your Word. Forgive me for when I have ignored it and instead
used the mirror of the world. Enable me to look carefully into
Your mirror and act on what I see there. Amen.*

Day One
Wardrobe Workout

1. For what purposes do you use your mirror? Do you usually like the reflection you see or do you tend to avoid mirrors? Discuss your love/hate relationship with your mirror.

2. How do societal mirrors in the media affect your self-image? Do images of successful people, gorgeous movie stars, or perfectly decorated homes change the view you have of yourself?

3. The verses we read in the Book of James tell us that we are to use God's Word as our mirror. Let's learn more about this spiritual mirror. Read Psalm 19:7–11. (Remember that words such as *law*, *testimony*, and *precepts* all refer to God's Word.)

   a. What are some characteristics of our spiritual mirror, God's Word?

b. What can God's Word do for us?

c. Compare Psalm 19:11 with James 1:25. According to these two verses, what are three or four ways we can use God's mirror in order to gain its benefits?

4. What key lesson did you learn today?

5. Our memory verse for this week is 2 Corinthians 3:18 (NIV): "And we, who with unveiled faces all reflect the Lord's glory, are being transformed into His like-ness with ever-increasing glory, which comes from the Lord, who is the Spirit." To help you memorize this verse, write it out in the space below.

Day Two
◇◇◇◇◇◇◇◇◇◇◇◇◇◇◇◇
False Mirrors

You have put off the old self with its practices
and have put on the new self, which is being
renewed in knowledge after the image of its creator.
Colossians 3:9–10

Three-way mirrors. Rearview mirrors. Fun-house mirrors. These may all give us false reflections.

There are other mirrors that we should avoid. In this Bible study, we have been looking at the unattractive garments in our attitude closets and weeding them out. These same attitudes and behaviors can be compared to mirrors. Let's review them.

Surveillance mirror. Perhaps you've noticed these convex mirrors hanging near the ceilings of convenience stores. Their curved shape allows the attendants to have a full view of the store. Similarly, Control uses the surveillance mirror to make sure everyone is doing what she thinks they are supposed to be doing. If they aren't, she'll let them know. However, now that we have taken off that field marshal uniform, we don't need this mirror. We have given control to God, surrendered our rights to Him, and allowed Him to lead. We have given up on controlling others; they also report to our Commander-in-Chief.

Purse mirror. This is the mirror Worry uses. She carries it in her bag wherever she goes. This mirror helps her frequently check on her anxieties. Often, this is a magnifying mirror as well, making her cares and concerns look larger than they really are. She turns to this mirror every chance she gets. Now that we have given God our macramé bag of worries, we find that we really don't miss that little mirror. Life is much more pleasant when we trust in God's love and provision, seek His king- dom, and live one day at a time. We're learning to retrain our minds and experience Christ's peace.

Vanity mirror. Every woman needs one of these to check on her hair and make- up, but Pride spends too much time admiring herself in the vanity mirror. Pride is enamored with her reflection, her image, and her importance. The reflection we saw while wearing the prom dress of pride appeared attractive, but now we see that the clothing of humility is much more pleasing to our divine Designer. We have taken off those attention-getting ruffles, the hoop-skirt of superiority, and the corset of conceit. We are finding practical ways to wear humility, such as praising God, honoring others, serving without reward, and embracing humbling experiences. We just don't need that vanity mirror anymore.

Two-way mirror. If you watch crime dramas, you will see the police using two-way mirrors when interrogating the bad guys. While one officer is questioning the suspect in one room, other law-enforcement officials are watching in another room behind the two-way mirror. The suspect does not see the people in the other room, but they can watch him. Envy uses this mirror to look at what other people have, forgetting to look at the blessings she already possesses. Now that we have pitched our envy-green ensemble and are learning to wear the color of contentment, we don't need the two-way mirror. In fact, a regular mirror will do just fine as we learn to count our blessings. It will help us to avoid comparison and to reflect on our own blessings. We can now rejoice that God is enough. He will supply our needs and satisfy our desires.

Parabolic mirror. A concave-shaped parabolic mirror is sometimes used in telescopes. All of the light waves entering a parabolic mirror are focused on one point. Selfishness uses this mirror to focus everything on—you guessed it—self. Selfishness makes sure everything is centered on her. All attention and every situation converges on her person. But those focusing rays can become uncomfortable, so we're exchanging the parabolic mirror for a mirror that will reflect God's love to others. We are learning to embrace sacrifice and lay down our own timetables and preferences in order to serve others. We experience God's grace as He forgives our self-centeredness and gives us the strength to change.

Smoked mirror. Smoked mirror tiles give a classy, glossy appearance to any wall, but all the reflections are dark and gray. In the same way, the poison of bitterness darkens the soul. Everything Bitterness looks at is smoky and shadowy. Bitterness stores up all the hurtful images and the accompanying anger. Now that we have allowed God to unravel the bitterness sweater and chosen to wear soft-as-cashmere forgiveness, we can see clearly. The smoky shadows vanish as God brightens our outlook. As we choose to forgive, God gives us the grace to do so. He transforms the pain into a new purpose for our lives.

We are learning to follow the apostle Paul's instructions to the Colossians to "put off the old self" (Colossians 3:9). We have stripped off those uncomfortable, unattractive garments, realizing that it's time to clean the closets. While we're at it, we'll get rid of all those misleading mirrors too. We thought they would bring happiness and make us look like a million dollars, but instead they only brought anxiety and made us miserable.

Now we can "put on the new self" (v. 10). God transforms us through renewal of our minds. By giving us a new mirror, His Word, He changes our attitudes, alters our thoughts, and adjusts our mind-set. As we allow God to strip off controlling behavior, worry, and pride, we resemble more closely the pure and holy being the Father intended us to be. When envy, selfishness, and bitterness are thrown away, we come closer to the image God designed for us.

Dear Jesus, help me to avoid all the false mirrors around me such as the mirrors that focus all the attention on others' faults or their blessings and the mirrors that concentrate on my worries or my importance. Use the mirror of Your Word to renew the spirit of my mind. Amen.

Day Two
Wardrobe Workout

1. Of the mirrors discussed in this chapter, which is your favorite one to use? Why do you tend to hang on to this one?

2. Match the mirrors with the appropriate memory verse from chapters 2–7. See if you can do this without looking back through the book.

Surveillance mirror	a. 1 John 3:16
Purse mirror	b. Philippians 4:6–7
Vanity mirror	c. 1 Peter 5:5
Two-way mirror	d. Psalm 40:8
Parabolic mirror	e. Colossians 3:12–13
Smoked mirror	f. Philippians 4:12–13

In the space below, write out the verse that corresponds to your answer to question number one. How can this verse help you to get rid of that mirror?

3. What key lesson did you learn today?

4. Write out our memory verse for this week: "And we, who with unveiled faces all reflect the Lord's glory, are being transformed into His likeness with ever-increasing glory, which comes from the Lord, who is the Spirit" (2 Corinthians 3:18 NIV). Write it out phrase by phrase, trying to do as much of it as you can by memory.

Day Three

◇◇◇◇◇◇◇◇◇◇◇◇◇◇◇◇◇◇◇◇◇◇◇◇

She's Got the Look

You are all sons of God through faith in Christ Jesus, for all of you
who were baptized into Christ have clothed yourselves with Christ.
Galatians 3:26–27 NIV

On the television show *What Not to Wear*, the hosts, Stacy and Clinton, have a certain image in mind for the makeover participant. They tailor an attractive wardrobe to each person's profession, personality, and body type. The fashion experts display three ideal sample outfits and explain why these clothes would be attractive on that individual. They tell her which styles to avoid and which fashions will make her image shine.

What exactly is the image God has planned for us? Romans 8:29 describes the design:

> For those whom He foreknew He also predestined to be conformed
> to the image of His Son, in order that He might be the firstborn
> among many brothers.

The look God designs for us is the image of Christ! Our dear Father wants us all to have the likeness of His Son. We will all have a family resemblance. In fact, Galatians 3:27 (NIV) says we "have clothed [ourselves] with Christ."

What does it mean to put on Christ? When we dress in clothing, it covers us. When people look at us, they see the garment, not our skin. When we put on Christ, He will be the one that others see. Our own faults are not as obvious when they are covered with the graciousness of Christ.

An expert wardrobe consultant will be able to select clothing that will hide your figure flaws. Got large hips? Wear a loose-leg pant in a dark color. Full bust? A V-neckline will be very flattering. Want to hide a tummy? Try a ruched waistline that hits you just beneath your bust.

Just as each of us may struggle with a specific body problem, we will also have different spiritual struggles. I most often wrestle with the issue of control. For you, worry may be more of a problem. Perhaps bitterness is your main spiritual dilemma. The wonderful thing about clothing ourselves with Christ is that His righteousness covers any and all flaws!

When we are clothed with Christ, people will recognize that we belong to Him. Certain professions have clothing that helps us recognize their roles. Medical personnel wear scrubs. Policemen wear dark-blue uniforms. Businessmen wear tailored suits, button-down shirts, and power ties. Oh, and hula dancers wear grass skirts. Other people will recognize our role as a child of God because they will see that the clothing of our attitudes is different. We resemble Christ in our kindness, goodness, patience, forgiveness, service, and love.

Being clothed with Christ is not just playing dress-up. When we put on Christ, He changes us from the inside out. Martin Luther tells us:

> In those who have been baptized a new light and flame arise; new
> and devout emotions come into being, such as fear and trust in God
> and hope; and a new will emerges. This is what it means to put on
> Christ properly, truly, and according to the Gospel. . . . For when we
> have put on Christ, the garment of our righteousness and salvation,
> then we also put on Christ, the garment of imitation. (LW 26:352–
> 53)

Outwardly, we are imitating Christ, while inwardly, He is changing our spirits and giving us His wisdom, holiness, and power.

A wardrobe consultant will carefully select the right clothes for each individual client. She chooses garments based on the personality and lifestyle of the individual as well as the body type and coloring of each person. The new styles are designed to coax them out of their rut and give them a new fashion sense.

Some clients will strive to follow the new style suggestions, even if they are totally out of their usual fashion realm. Other participants, however, immediately revert to their old style. A bohemian at heart continues to select oversized, brightly-colored skirts instead of a classy business suit. The girl with the Goth look persists in buying black when she really needs some vivid colors. The mom who wears her comfortable sweats day in and day out buys another baggy sweatshirt instead of the recommended fitted jacket.

How often do I do that as well? My heavenly Wardrobe Consultant has shown me the look that would be the most flattering for me: Christ's image. However, I am tempted to revert to my old, comfortable styles. God says, "Here, let Me take that heavy bag of worries. It's truly wreaking havoc on your posture." I agree, but I still go right back to the rack of bulky knotted purses. Christ suggests a color change: "Envy-green is really not your color." I see the difference that the color of contentment makes, but I am still drawn to the racks of olive slacks, emerald sweaters, or lime-green T-shirts. The Spirit asks, "Aren't those boots of selfishness uncomfortable?" and I gladly give them up for a time, yet almost the next instant, they are my footwear of choice.

When a fashion client is veering from new wardrobe rules, the television consultant rushes in to save the day. She patiently shows the individual some attractive options that follow the guidelines. She explains why the new fashions are better than the old.

The Holy Spirit does this for us as well. When we are tempted to return to our old styles of controlling behavior, pride, or bitterness, He works through Word and Sacrament and through the example and guidance of other Christians to remind us that those fashions are passé. He will show us new ways to wear surrender, humility, and forgiveness. He will encourage us when it seems too difficult to give up the clothing to which we've become accustomed.

Gradually, it becomes easier to leave our old fashion choices behind and become more consistent in getting the right look. Our Wardrobe Consultant is with us every day. Our style manual, the Bible, is always available. Of course, there are times when we will forget to consult the style manual or refuse to listen to our divine

Designer, but as we grow in faith, we will develop the look we're after: the image of Christ.

> *Dear Father, now I know the image You want me to have: the image of Christ. Forgive me when I continue in my old patterns. Change me from the inside out. May everyone recognize Christ in me. In His name. Amen.*

Day Three
◇◇◇◇◇◇◇◇◇◇◇◇◇◇◇◇◇◇◇◇◇◇◇◇◇◇◇◇
Wardrobe Workout

1. When a fashion client is having difficulties following her fashion guidelines, the wardrobe consultant will help and encourage. The Holy Spirit does the same for us when we are struggling to achieve the image God has designed for us. How has our heavenly Wardrobe Consultant helped you in your spiritual make-over?

2. The look we're after is the image of Christ. What does that image look like? Read the following passages to discover some characteristics of Christ:

   Matthew 9:10–13 _____

   _____

Matthew 9:36 _____

_____

Matthew 11:29 _____

_____

Mark 1:35 _____

_____

Mark 10:43–45 _____

_____

Luke 23:34 _____

_____

John 5:30 _____

_____

Circle one characteristic you would like to see more of in your own life.

3. What key lesson did you learn today?

4. Write out this week's memory verse. Try not to peek.

Day Four
◇◇◇◇◇◇◇◇◇◇◇◇◇◇◇◇◇◇◇
Your Mirror, Lord

And we, who with unveiled faces all reflect the Lord's glory, are
being transformed into His likeness with ever-increasing glory,
which comes from the Lord, who is the Spirit.
2 Corinthians 3:18 NIV

Remember the story about my singing group days spent traveling in good old Miracle White (p. 62)? I have many fond recollections of that eventful year, but one of my first memories is of James, our keyboardist, playing a song he had written. It instantly became my favorite. Even now, it is sort of an anthem for my life. That song is titled "Mirror":

> *I long to be Your mirror, Lord*
> *I pray that You will be*
> *the one who will be noticed*
> *when people look at me.*
> *They'll see You . . . Jesus.*
> *("Mirror," James Werning)*

What a beautiful picture of Christian life.

I truly desire to reflect Christ and to function as a mirror that displays His mercy and love. When I do, the focus is on Jesus, not on me. Part of my nature wants all the attention to be directed at me, me, me. Ultimately, this is not satisfying. One of the great paradoxes of the Christian life is that I am more fulfilled when I'm small and God is great. As I direct attention away from myself toward my Savior, I experience my greatest purpose: to bring honor to God.

Paul used the image of a mirror in 2 Corinthians 3:18 (NIV):

> And we, who with unveiled faces all reflect the Lord's glory, are being transformed into His likeness with ever-increasing glory, which comes from the Lord, who is the Spirit.

Paul says that we "are being transformed" into His likeness. As we look at the Lord's glory, we experience a true makeover into the image of Christ. Paul writes that we "*are being* transformed" (emphasis added): we ourselves do not do the actual makeover. Only God can change our hearts. However, we need to respond to His gracious calling. We need to nominate ourselves for the spiritual *What Not to Wear* show and allow the Spirit to work in our lives, changing our wardrobes.

We "are being transformed" with increasing degrees of glory. It is a continuous process. Our makeover will not be complete until we are in heaven. When we received the gift of faith in Baptism, we were given the robe of righteousness, which is the beginning of our makeover. As we progress, our character begins to match our pristine robe.

How is this process accomplished?

During a concert one night, my friend James related how he was inspired to write the song "Mirror." One warm, sunny autumn day, he was hiking in the Black Hills of South Dakota, where he discovered a large piece of mica on the ground. Mica is a rock made up of many thin, glass-like layers compressed together. The upper layers were cracked and dirty. He began peeling off some of the soiled, dusty pieces and was surprised by a sheen that he had not suspected under all that dirt. As he continued to remove more layers, the glassy plates became clearer. Finally, the removal process revealed a surface that had been hidden deep in the rock but which now shone as a brilliant mirror.

James observed that our lives are often like the dirty mica, lacking the beauty that God intended us to have. Our Lord is patiently waiting for us to allow Him to peel away the impure layers of our lives so that He can restore our polish and sheen. Then we will become mirrors, reflecting the life of Jesus into a darkened world.

When Christ strips away the film of our old nature and the deposit of dirt left by the world, He transforms us into the mirror we were meant to be. The process is not always painless. Like a little child who does not want to take a bath, we are reluctant to shed our layers of filth. Sometimes the Lord wants to peel away something we think is important in our life, something we perceive as essential to happiness. But when we submit to the procedure, we discover joy in Him, not mere happiness with ourselves. Just as James discovered a beautiful mirror beneath the dirty layers of mica, so we discover our true selves when we allow God to peel away what is getting in the way of reflecting Him. Our authentic form will appear when Jesus has sloughed off all the grimy, unnecessary deposits that cover our lives. Only then can we truly shine in His glory.

Do you long to be a mirror of the Lord? Allow Him to peel away the layers that are preventing your true self from shining. Look into Jesus' face and reflect His love to the world.

Dear Lord, I do long to be Your mirror. I pray that when people look at me, all they see is You. Peel away any layers of my old nature that are getting in the way of reflecting Your grace. Amen.

Day Four
◇◇◇◇◇◇◇◇◇◇◇◇◇◇◇◇◇◇◇◇◇◇
Wardrobe Workout

1. How are our lives here on earth like the piece of mica that my friend James found?

2. In 1 Corinthians 13:12, we read, "For now we see in a mirror dimly, but then face to face. Now I know in part; then I shall know fully, even as I have been fully known." Think back on times in your life when you were confused about the direction in which God was leading you. Upon reflection, how do you see His hand at work in your life during that time?

3. What key lesson did you learn today?

4. Write out the memory verse for the week. No peeking!

◇◇◇◇◇◇◇◇◇◇◇◇
Study Styles

Studying a person in the Bible is an excellent method to glean life-changing truth from God's Word. Fortunately, God included many stories of men and women who followed Him. The stories reveal not only their love and devotion to God but also their faults and shortcomings.

Because we have been studying the transforming power of a relationship with God, let's examine the story of a woman who experienced a radical transformation through a brief meeting with Jesus. Her tale is told in John 4. Jesus was traveling from the southern part of Israel, called Judea, to the northern region of Galilee. Between these two areas was the region of Samaria, which Jewish travelers normally avoided by traveling on the east side of the Jordan River. Jews considered Samaritans unclean because in past centuries they had intermarried with non-Jews. Jews did not associate with Samaritans; they would certainly not eat or drink together.

Jesus arrived at the well of Sychar at about noon. There, He met a woman coming to get water, even though people usually drew water in the evening in order to avoid the heat of the day. Read John 4:1–42 to discover Jesus' encounter with this Samaritan woman.

Would you agree that this woman experienced a spiritual makeover? What spiritual clothing did she wear before she met Jesus? How did Jesus change her? In the following chart, write down characteristics of her life and personality before and after their meeting. The account does not specifically name her character qualities, but put yourself in the culture of the day. Try to feel her emotions and see her through Jesus' eyes. Include verse references. I have done one example for you.

Before Meeting Jesus	After Meeting Jesus
Thirsty: physically (v. 7) and spiritually (vv. 11, 25).	No longer thirsty (v. 28) .

With which characteristic or emotion of the Samaritan woman do you most identify?

How can her encounter with Jesus help you to experience transformation in this area?

Write a three-step action plan to work on this area of your life.

Example: Lately I have been feeling thirsty, sensing my life is lacking something. The Samaritan woman's story shows me I need more of the living water: Jesus.

In order to obtain more living water:

1) I will go to the well (God's Word) daily.
2) Specifically, I will read the Gospel of John.
3) As I read, I will write down ways that Jesus satisfied people's needs.

Day Five

◇◇◇◇◇◇◇◇◇◇◇◇◇◇◇

Mirror, Mirror

Therefore, if anyone is in Christ, he is a new creation.
The old has passed away; behold, the new has come.
2 Corinthians 5:17

"Mirror, mirror on the wall, who's the fairest of them all?" Do you remember those words spoken by the evil queen in the fairy tale *Snow White and the Seven Dwarfs*? Each time the queen approached the mirror, she fully expected the mirror to reply, "You, O queen, are the fairest of them all." Watch out if this was not the answer she received! If the mirror mentioned anyone else, the unfortunate beauty was quickly done away with so that the next day the queen would receive the reply she wanted from the magic mirror.

The queen is a fictional character, but her longings are based in reality. We all want to be desirable, attractive, and sought after. Who wouldn't want a mirror that gave a daily dose of admiration?

God has a magic mirror of His own. In this looking glass, God sees us not as we are, but as we will be. The Bible tells us, "If anyone is in Christ, he is a new creation" (2 Corinthians 5:17).

When God looks at us in His miraculous mirror, He already perceives us as fair and beautiful because He sees us dressed in our robes of Christ's righteousness. He sees the spiritual makeover complete.

In her book *Every Thought Captive*, Jerusha Clark writes about God's perspective:

> Unlimited by time, He can view us as we are and as we will be. His perception of us is not based on isolated moments, nor does He see us only against the backdrop of our past. Instead, God knows who we are *right now*—a new creation—and who we are *becoming*—the sanctified bride of His beloved Son. (Clark, p. 37)

In God's eyes, we are already beautiful. He sees us forgiven, pure, and perfected. A trained fashion consultant is able to look at the "before" picture of a makeover nominee and see a stylish graduate of Fashion University. She can see past baggy, stretched-out sweats, grimy sneakers, and split ends to envision a polished woman in a chic suit, stylish pumps, and a fresh 'do. God can also look beyond our frumpy faults and our dated deficiencies and visualize a pure, lovely, and new creation.

Yes, while we are on earth, the new creation is not complete. God desires us to allow Him to peel away the grime from our lives to reveal His perfect handiwork. He also longs for us to hear His words of love and acceptance.

We can see ourselves in God's miraculous mirror by looking in His Word. In it, God tells us over and over how much He loves us and how precious we are to Him. When I am feeling unloved and unlovely, I can look in God's miraculous mirror to see who I am in His eyes. In His Word, God tells me I am:

- Beautiful: "All beautiful you are, my darling; there is no flaw in you" (Song of Songs 4:7 NIV). My Creator sees me as perfected in Christ and flawless in His eyes. In Jesus, I am lovely.
- A delight: "The LORD delights in those who fear Him, who put their hope in His unfailing love" (Psalm 147:11 NIV). Amazing! God finds happiness and pleasure in me.
- His bride: "As the bridegroom rejoices over the bride, so shall your God rejoice over you" (Isaiah 62:5). My Lord perceives me as a lovely, pure bride. Our relationship brings Him joy.
- A reason to rejoice: "The LORD your God is in your midst, a mighty one who will save; He will rejoice over you with gladness; He will quiet you by His love; He will exult over you with loud singing" (Zephaniah 3:17). I love these word pictures as I imagine God singing joyful songs with my name, beaming with delight as He looks at me, and soothing my doubts with His faithful love.
- Precious, honored, and loved: "Because you are precious in My eyes, and honored, and I love you, I give men in return for you, peoples in exchange for your life" (Isaiah 43:4). I am precious to God, valuable in His sight, treasured in His kingdom, and cherished in His heart.
- Lavished with love: "How great is the love the Father has lavished on us, that we should be called children of God! And that is what we are!" (1 John 3:1 NIV). God is not stingy with His love. He lavishes it on us extravagantly!

Let us rejoice in the fact that our Lord sees us in His miraculous mirror as precious, treasured, and beautiful. Let's bask in His joy, delight, and love. Let's appreciate our positions as His bride, friend, daughter, and chosen one.

When we know we are loved, we can trust the One who loves us. We can trust that He knows what He is doing when He is sloughing off our rough spots so that we can shine. We can ask Him to help us see the culmination of our makeover and cooperate with the Spirit as He works on our wardrobes. Let the Lord take control. Give Him worry and develop trust. Throw away the prom dress of pride and accept the clothing of humility. Forget about wearing envy-green and allow Christ to clothe you with the color of contentment. Give up on selfishness and put on the shoes of love and sacrifice. Let Jesus unravel your bitterness and give you His grace to forgive.

Our spiritual makeover will not be truly complete until we see Jesus face to face. But even now, we will begin to gleam as we look to our Savior and reflect His beauty. We can experience the true joy of functioning as a mirror that reveals Jesus. We can celebrate the fact that our Creator sees our renovation complete. Even now, we can experience freedom and authenticity as the Holy Spirit pulls away the layers of grime that encrust our lives so that we can shine.

Jesus has started our spiritual makeover. Let's participate fully in His means of grace—His Word and Sacraments—and allow Him to work out His vision for our lives!

> O dear Father, thank You for the grace that covers me so that You see me not only as I am but also as I will be. Continue to work a spiritual makeover in my heart until I am in heaven with You. In Jesus' name. Amen.

Day Five
◇◇◇◇◇◇◇◇◇◇◇◇◇◇◇◇◇◇◇◇◇◇◇◇◇◇
Wardrobe Workout

1. Discuss your reaction to the words, "God can also look beyond our frumpy faults and our dated deficiencies and visualize a pure, lovely, and new creation" (p. 199).

2. The chapter listed verses that tell us how God sees us. Which verse meant the most to you? Why?

3. What key lesson did you learn today?

4. Write out 2 Corinthians 3:18 from memory.

Meaningful Makeover

Think back over our whole makeover experience. In cleaning out our closets, we have tossed out unattractive garments and made way for Christ to clothe us in a more God-pleasing fashion.

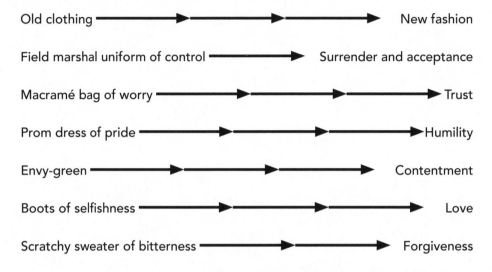

Old clothing ➤➤➤ New fashion

Field marshal uniform of control ➤ Surrender and acceptance

Macramé bag of worry ➤➤➤ Trust

Prom dress of pride ➤➤➤ Humility

Envy-green ➤➤➤ Contentment

Boots of selfishness ➤➤➤ Love

Scratchy sweater of bitterness ➤➤ Forgiveness

In which area have you experienced the biggest transformation? What principles did you learn that helped you to change?

Which area still needs some work?

Don't despair. Our spiritual makeover will not be complete until we reach heaven. Remember that the Holy Spirit gently removes the dingy grime from our lives layer by layer. Each time a layer is removed, we will reflect our Savior better. Our biggest challenge is in being willing to nominate ourselves for God's makeover show. Write a prayer asking the Holy Spirit to give you the desire to be changed into Christ's image. Ask Him to take away the stained layer you mentioned above and to show you your part in the process. Write the prayer on a card to carry with you and pray it daily. Include a Bible verse from our study that can help you in this area.

Parting Words

God wants every person to possess the garment of salvation. He gives this garment freely because Jesus, His Son, already paid the price through His perfect life, death, and resurrection. When the Holy Spirit empowers you to believe that Jesus died and rose again for you, He gives you that essential garment of salvation.

God loves you and has a plan for you to know Him. He tells us this plan in the Bible, His Word to us.

- "For all have sinned and fall short of the glory of God" (Romans 3:23). No one is perfect. We all fail to meet God's standard of sinlessness. This sin prevents us from coming to Him and from entering heaven.
- "For God so loved the world, that He gave His only Son, that whoever believes in Him should not perish but have eternal life" (John 3:16). God loved us so much that He sent His own Son to take the punishment we deserved for our sins and mistakes. Jesus' death enables us to live with God forever.
- "For by grace you have been saved through faith. And this is not your own doing; it is the gift of God" (Ephesians 2:8). God gives us faith to believe in Jesus. His grace and mercy save us from death.
- "But to all who did receive Him, who believed in His name, He gave the right to become children of God" (John 1:12). By receiving Jesus in the waters of Baptism and the Holy Word of God, we become part of God's family.

I invite you to pray this prayer to the God who loves you and wants you to be part of His family:

Father in heaven, I realize that I am a sinner and fall short of what You want for my life. I know that I cannot save myself or earn eternal life. Thank You for sending Your Son, Jesus, to die for me. Through the power of His resurrection, You have made me alive eternally. Help me to turn from my sins and follow You. Thank You that although I may still fail, You will forgive me because Jesus paid the price for my sins. Thank You for Your gift of faith in Jesus, my Savior, and for the promise of eternal life with You. In Jesus' name I pray. Amen.

Through God's free gift of faith in Jesus, you possess the garment of salvation. You have the robe of righteousness and life forever with God. He has begun a spiritual makeover in you!

Amen and amen!

<<><><><><><><><><><><><><><><><><><><><><><><><><><><><><><><><><><><><><><>>

Appendix

<<><><><><><><><><><><><><><><><><><><><><><><><><><><><>>

Answers to Bible Study Questions

Week ONE, Day One

1. Answers will vary. 2. Answers will vary. 3. Answers will vary. 4. Memory verse.

Week ONE, Day Two

1. Answers will vary. 2. Ephesians 4:22–32: a. Answers will vary. b. Answers will vary. c. *Deceitful* can be defined as "not honest or having a tendency to deceive." To be deceitful is to cause someone else to accept as true what is actually false. A *desire* is a conscious impulse toward something that promises enjoyment or satisfaction in its attainment. Desires are longings or cravings. 3. Answers will vary. 4. Memory verse.

Week ONE, Day Three

1. Answers will vary. 2. a. Job 29:14: righteousness, justice; b. Psalm 30:11: joy or gladness; c. Isaiah 52:1: strength, splendor or beautiful garments; d. Luke 24:49: power. 3. Answers will vary. 4. Memory verse.

Week ONE, Day Four

1. Answers will vary. 2. Answers will vary. 3. Answers will vary. 4. Memory verse. **Study Styles:** What Not to Wear: old self, falsehood, anger, stealing, corrupt or unwholesome talk, bitterness, wrath, clamor, slander, malice. What to Wear: new self, truthful speech, honest work, speech that builds up others, kindness, tenderness or compassion, forgiveness. Other answers will vary.

Week ONE, Day Five

1. Answers will vary. 2. Answers will vary. 3. Answers will vary. 4. Memory verse. **Meaningful Makeover:** Answers will vary.

Week TWO, Day One

1. Answers will vary. 2. Answers will vary. 3. 1 Samuel 15:22: Obedience pleases God more than sacrifices. Isaiah 48:18: If we pay attention to God's commands, we will have peace and righteousness in abundance. Jeremiah 7:23: Obeying God's commands and following His ways will show we are His people; God gives us His commands for our good. John 14:21: Obeying God's commands shows Him that we love Him and will lead to a closer relationship with Him. 1 John 5:3: Keeping God's commands shows that we love Him; His commands are meant to bless our lives and therefore are not burdensome. 4. Answers will vary. 5. Memory verse.

Week TWO, Day Two

1. Answers will vary. 2. Romans 12:1–13: a. God asks that we present ourselves as living sacrifices, holy and acceptable to God. b. The first steps in becoming a living sacrifice are not conforming to the world around us and allowing God to transform us by renewing our minds. c. We begin to live a life of sacrifice by humbly using the gifts that God has given us to help the body of Christ: fellow believers. We can serve through speaking the Word of God (prophecy), serving, teaching, encouraging or exhorting others, generously contributing to the Church and to those in financial need, leading other Christians enthusiastically, and cheerfully helping others. We can also love one another, show each other honor, and not be lazy. We can endure with hope and patience when things are tough, praying for each other. Giving to those in need and practicing hospitality are also practical ways to serve. d. Answers will vary. 3. Answers will vary. 4. Memory verse.

Week TWO, Day Three

1. Answers will vary. 2. Exodus 15:13: Answers may include: God leads the people He has redeemed; He does not leave them on their own; God leads us with a love that will never quit; God leads us to heaven, His holy dwelling. 3. Answers will vary. 4. Memory verse.

Week TWO, Day Four

1. Answers will vary. 2. Answers will vary. 3. Answers will vary. 4. Memory verse. **Study Styles:** *Live:* Answers may include "act out, practice"; *Sinful:* Answers may include "full of sin, wicked, erring, immoral"; *Nature:* Answers may include "the inherent character of a person"; *Desire:* Answers may include "longing, want, wish, craving"; *Mind:* Answers may include "intellect, purpose, intentions"; *Death:* Answers may include "end of life, loss of life"; *Control:* Answers may include "exercise directing influence over, authority, have power over"; *Peace:* Answers may include "state of tranquility, serenity, calmness."

Week TWO, Day Five

1. Answers will vary. 2. Answers will vary. 3. Answers will vary. 4. Memory verse. **Meaningful Makeover:** Answers will vary.

Week THREE, Day One

1. Answers will vary. 2. Matthew 13:3–9, 18–23: a. Verse 22: Answers will vary. b. "Cares of the world," "weeds of worry": Thinking about money and the things of the world will occupy our minds, often shutting out thoughts of God; worrying puts the focus on what we can or cannot do and not on what God can do. c. Answers will vary. 3. Answers will vary. 4. Memory verse.

Week THREE, Day Two

1. Distraction and distrust; other answers will vary. 2. Psalm 9:10: God will not leave or forsake those who seek and trust Him. Psalm 32:10: God's steadfast and unfailing love will surround those who trust the Lord. Psalm 56:3–4: When we trust God, our fears are erased. Proverbs 3:5–6: When we trust in the Lord, He will make our paths straight (this can also mean that He will direct and lead us). 3. Answers will vary. 4. Memory verse.

Week THREE, Day Three

1. Answers will vary. 2. John 16:33: a. Jesus wants us to have peace. Jesus' peace is not dependent on circumstances. It is calm in the midst of a storm. It is beyond understanding. b. Jesus tells us that in this world we can expect trouble and tribulation. When we are wondering "Why me?" we can realize that problems are normal for this life. No one is given a pain-free life on this earth. c. "Jesus has already conquered the world and its problems." 3. Answers will vary. 4. Memory verse.

Week THREE, Day Four

1. Answers will vary. 2. Answers will vary. 3. Answers will vary. 4. Memory verse. **Study Styles:** Isaiah 26: Answers will vary, but might include: **Promise:** verse 3, "You will keep him in perfect peace"; **Example:** verse 10, an example not to follow: the wicked don't learn righteousness, even though God shows them grace; **Attitude:** verse 8, an attitude of desiring glory for God's name; **Command:** verse 4, "trust in the LORD forever"; **Enlargement** of my view of God: verse 12, all that we have accomplished is actually God working through us.

Week THREE, Day Five

1. Answers will vary. 2. Answers will vary. 3. Answers will vary. 4. Memory verse. **Meaningful Makeover:** Answers will vary.

Week FOUR, Day One

1. Answers will vary. 2. a. Proverbs 11:2: Pride brings disgrace or dishonor; b. Proverbs 29:23: Pride will actually bring a person low; c. Isaiah 2:17: Pride and haughtiness will result in being brought low and humbled; other answers will vary. 3. Answers will vary. 4. Memory verse.

◇◇

Week FOUR, Day Two

1. Answers will vary. 2. 2 Chronicles 26: a. Uzziah was sixteen years old when he became king. Zechariah instructed him in the fear of the Lord. God gave him success. Uzziah did what was right in the eyes of the Lord. b. King Uzziah won wars against the Philistines, the Arabians, the Meunites, and the Ammonites. He built and new towers, dug many cisterns, and had large fields and herds. He had a large army of 307,500 soldiers. He was successful because he was marvelously helped by God. c. Verse 16: Uzziah's pride led to his downfall. His pride was manifested through the act of entering the temple and burning incense to the Lord. This was wrong because only priests were allowed to burn incense to the Lord. Perhaps pride propelled him to that action because he had been so successful that he felt he could do anything. d. Verse 23: The eulogies at his funeral were short: "He had leprosy"; other answers will vary. 3. Answers will vary. 4. Memory verse.

Week FOUR, Day Three

1. Answers will vary. 2. Philippians 2:1–11: a. Verses 1–5: We can exhibit humility by considering others more significant than ourselves. We can examine our motives: are we doing what we are doing out of conceit? We can consider the interests of other people, not just our own. b. Verses 6–8: Christ did not consider equality with God something to be grasped; He did not demand the honor or privileges that He deserved. He made Himself nothing; He always had His majesty, but He did not always use it or demonstrate it. He willingly became a servant. He was obedient even to the point of death. c. Answers will vary. d. Verses 9–11: God exalted Him to the highest place and gave Him the highest name. One day, everyone will bow to Jesus and proclaim Him Lord. 4. Answers will vary. 5. Memory verse.

Week FOUR, Day Four

1. Answers will vary. 2. Answers will vary. 3. Answers will vary. 4. Memory verse. **Study Styles:** Deuteronomy 8:2: God may humble us to test our hearts for obedience. 2 Chronicles 7:14: When we humble ourselves, seek God, and repent of our sins, God hears and forgives. Psalm 25:9: God leads and teaches those who are humble. Proverbs 3:34: God gives grace and favor to the humble. Daniel 4:37: God is able to humble all those who walk in pride. Ephesians 4:2: God wants us to be completely humble and gentle. James 4:10: If we humble ourselves before the Lord, He will exalt us and lift us up.

Week FOUR, Day Five

1. Ephesians 6:5–8: a. Attitudes toward service could include serving others with respect, serving sincerely and wholeheartedly, not serving only when people are looking, and doing your work as if you were serving the Lord. b. Paul tells us that God will reward us for whatever good we do. 2. Answers will vary. 3. Memory verse. **Meaningful Makeover:** Answers will vary.

Week FIVE, Day One

1. Answers will vary. 2. James 3:13–18: a. Verse 14: We often display envy by boasting. Conversely, we might also deny it: "be false to the truth." b. Verse 15: Envy or jealousy is not the wisdom from above. It "is earthly, unspiritual, demonic." c. Verse 16: Jealousy and envy lead to disorder and evil practices or habits. d. Verses 13, 17: God's wisdom is humble and meek. It is "first pure, then peaceable, gentle, open to reason, full of mercy and good fruits, impartial and sincere." 3. Answers will vary. 4. Memory verse.

◇◇

Week FIVE, Day Two

1. Answers will vary. 2. Psalm 73: a. Verse 3: Asaph's envy was caused by seeing the prosperity of the wicked. b. Verses 4–12: Asaph saw those he envied as having no troubles. He thought they were proud and violent. Their hearts were hard or foolish. He thought they were carefree and wealthy and that they didn't even think God knew what they were doing. Other answers will vary. c. Verses 2, 13–16, 21–22: Envy caused Asaph to stumble because he felt that he had wasted his life trying to be good when the wicked people around him seemed to lead charmed lives. He became sad and bitter and gave God the silent treatment. Other answers will vary. d. Verses 17–20: Asaph's attitude was changed when he entered the sanctuary of God: when he entered God's presence. God showed him that those he envied would be swept away and that what he was envying would not last. Other answers will vary. e. Verses 3, 23–28: Contrast Asaph's desires in the beginning of the psalm with the end: In the beginning, Asaph was looking at the prosperity of the wicked and focusing on the things of the world. At the end, he was longing for God and no longer desiring what was on earth. Being near to God satisfied him. Other answers will vary. 3. Answers will vary. 4. Memory verse.

Week FIVE, Day Three

1. Answers will vary. 2. Genesis 30:9–24: a. *Gad* can mean "good fortune" or "a troop." *Asher* means "happy." *Issachar* sounds like the Hebrew for "reward." *Zebulun* probably means "honor." *Joseph* means "may he add." Leah still wants her husband's love and honor. She views her children as rewards for her behavior. She did say that she was happy when Asher was born, but it didn't last long. Rachel finally had a child of her own, but she named him, "May he add." She was not satisfied. It looks like each is still discontent with her situation and envious of the other sister. b. Answers will vary. 3. Answers will vary. 4. Memory verse.

Week FIVE, Day Four

1. a. Answers will vary. b. Answers for the definition of *contentment* may include feeling satisfaction with one's possessions, status, or situation. c. Answers will vary. d. Answers may include: The Lord gives us His body and blood. We are reminded of His forgiveness and refreshed by His presence. These give true contentment, which the world cannot offer. 2. Answers will vary. 3. Memory verse. **Study Styles:** Answers will vary.

Week FIVE, Day Five

1. a. Answers will vary. b. Answers will vary. 2. Colossians 3:2–5, 11: a. Answers may vary, but should include comments about those who have gifts of the Spirit, understanding of God's love in Jesus, and unity, while those who conform to the fallen world will lack theological understanding and will not receive eternal life. b. Answers will vary. 3. Answers will vary. 4. Memory verse. **Meaningful Makeover:** Answers will vary.

Week SIX, Day One

1. Answers will vary. 2. Answers for the definition of selfishness may include being concerned with your own interests and needs while ignoring those of others; showing that your own personal wishes are more important than those of other people. 3. Genesis 4:1–12: a. Perhaps God asked Cain this question because He wanted Cain to admit what he had done. God was giving him a chance to repent. b. Cain's response shows a self-centered attitude. He did not care about his brother. c. Answers will vary. d. Answers will vary. 4. Answers will vary. 5. Memory verse.

‹◊◊◊›

Week SIX, Day Two

1. Answers will vary. 2. Mark 10:34–45: a. Answers will vary. b. Verse 37: The request of James and John to sit at Jesus' right hand and left hand reveals their desire for positions of power and significance. Human nature tends to make everything all about itself. It displays self-centeredness, exhibits self-absorption, and desires self-importance. c. Verse 42: Jesus portrays man's attitude as one of superiority. In our natural self, we want to be served, to give orders, and to tell others what to do. Other answers will vary. d. If we follow Jesus, our attitudes and behaviors will no longer be characterized by selfishness but by service. Greatness in God's eyes is not superiority but servanthood. e. Jesus washed the disciples' dirty feet (John 13:1–17). As God, He could have chosen to be born to a rich, powerful family, but He chose to live a life of poverty (Matthew 8:20). Jesus healed many people, even at the end of a long day when He might have been exhausted and worn out (Mark 1:32–34). Other answers will vary. 3. Answers will vary. 4. Memory verse.

Week SIX, Day Three

1. Answers will vary. 2. 1 Corinthians 13: a. Shoes of love would be patient, kind, humble, polite, forgiving, and truthful. Shoes of love would defer to others. Shoes of love would be lasting. b. Answers will vary. c. Answers will vary. d. Answers will vary. 3. Answers will vary. 4. Memory verse.

Week SIX, Day Four

1. Answers will vary. 2. Answers will vary. 3. 1 John 3:1–3: a. It comes from the Father. b. Through the sacrament of Holy Baptism. c. Our hope is in Christ Jesus, who has freed us from slavery to sin. 4. Answers will vary. 5. Memory verse. **Study Styles:** Answers will vary.

Week SIX, Day Five

1. Answers will vary. 2. Answers will vary. 3. Memory verse. **Meaningful Make-over:** Answers will vary.

✕✕

Week SEVEN, Day One

1. Answers will vary. 2. Answers will vary. 3. Answers will vary. 4. Answers will vary. 5. Memory verse.

Week SEVEN, Day Two

1. Answers will vary. 2. Matthew 18:21–35. a. Answers will vary. b. Answers may include that Jesus wants us to keep on forgiving others. He wants us to forgive more times than we can count. c. Answers may include: The huge debt represents the debt I owe God for paying the price for my sin. There is no way that I can repay God. d. Answers will vary. e. The master called the unmerciful servant wicked. God views withholding forgiveness as evil, wicked, and wrong. f. The unmerciful servant was thrown into jail to be tortured. When we hang onto bitterness, our minds are imprisoned in a negative cycle and our thoughts are tortured. g. Answers will vary. 3. Answers will vary. 4. Memory verse.

Week SEVEN, Day Three

1. Answers will vary. 2. Job 14:16–17: God does not keep track of our sin. His forgiveness erases our record of wrongs. Psalm 103:11–12: God removes our sins as far as the east is from the west. His forgiveness means He no longer looks at our sins. Isaiah 43:25: God blots out our transgressions and does not remember them. God's forgiveness is complete. 3. Answers will vary. 4. Memory verse.

Week SEVEN, Day Four

1. Answers will vary. 2. Answers will vary. 3. Answers will vary. 4. Answers will vary. 5. Memory verse. **Study Styles:** Answers will vary.

◇◇

Week SEVEN, Day Five

1. Today's reading listed these five ways to cover an offense: 1. Refuse to repeat the matter. 2. Cover the offense in our minds and refuse to brood on the offense. 3. Cover the offense with God's Word. 4. Cover the offense with prayer. 5. Receive the strength to cover the offense by receiving forgiveness for your own sins through the Lord's Supper. Remaining answers will vary. 2. Answers will vary. 3. Answers will vary. 4. Memory verse. **Meaningful Makeover:** Answers will vary.

Week EIGHT, Day One

1. Answers will vary. 2. Answers will vary. 3. Psalm 19:7–11: a. God's Word, our spiritual mirror, is perfect, sure or trustworthy, right, clean or pure, and true. It endures forever. It is more desirable than gold or honey. (Answers will vary with different versions of the Bible.) b. God's Word revives our soul, makes us wise, and gives joy to our hearts. It enlightens us, warns us, and rewards us. c. Ways we can use God's mirror include looking intently into the mirror (studying God's Word), continually using the mirror, not forgetting what we read and learn from the mirror, and acting according to the mirror (doing what God's Word tells us to do). 4. Answers will vary. 5. Memory verse.

Week EIGHT, Day Two

1. Answers will vary. 2. Answers should line up this way: Surveillance mirror: d. Purse mirror: b. Vanity mirror: c. Two-way mirror: f. Parabolic mirror: a. Smoked mirror: e. Remaining answers will vary. 3. Answers will vary. 4. Memory verse.

Week EIGHT, Day Three

1. Answers will vary. 2. Matthew 9:10–13: Jesus associated with sinners. He was willing to hurt His own reputation in order to go to the people who needed Him. Matthew 9:36: Jesus is compassionate. Matthew 11:29: Jesus is gentle and humble. Mark 1:35: Jesus made time for prayer and fellowship with the Father a priority. Mark 10:43–45: Jesus came to serve. Luke 23:34: Jesus is forgiving. John 5:30: Jesus did not seek to please Himself; He wanted to please the Father. 3. Answers will vary. 4. Memory verse.

Week EIGHT, Day Four

1. Answers will vary. 2. Answers will vary. 3. Answers will vary. 4. Memory verse. **Study Styles:** Characteristics of the woman at the well before meeting Jesus could include: perhaps secretive, because she came to the well at an unusual time (v. 6); curious about Jesus and questioning Him (v. 9); searching for but not finding true love and relationships (vv. 17–18); defensive and prejudiced (vv. 19–20); looking for the Messiah (v. 25). Characteristics of the woman at the well after meeting Jesus could include: no longer secretive, because she was willing to admit to her past (v. 29); amazed at Jesus (v. 29), believing in Jesus as the Messiah (vv. 29, 39, 42); influential (vv. 39, 42); eager (v. 29). Remaining answers will vary.

Week EIGHT, Day Five

1. Answers will vary. 2. Answers will vary. 3. Answers will vary. 4. Memory verse. **Meaningful Makeover:** Answers will vary.